I GIVE YOU WINGS WITH

Lona Copeland-B

Faith Publishing
London, England

Unless otherwise noted, all Bible scriptures are quoted from the King James Version. Please note that the name satan is not capitalised. I have chosen not to acknowledge him, even to the point of violating grammatical rules.

1st Edition

I GIVE YOU WINGS WITH WHICH TO FLY

Lona Copeland-Blake

ISBN: 0-9540966-0-6
Copyright ' 2001
Lona Copeland-Blake
28 Brunswick Court
London SE1 3LX

Published by Faith Publishing
28 Brunswick Court
London SE1 3LX
email: pastor_lona_copeland@hotmail.com

Printed in the England by Clays Ltd, St. Ives plc. Cover design by ministryinart.com. All rights reserved under international copyright law. The contents of this book may not be reproduced whether in whole or in part, without the written consent of the publisher.

Contents

v. Dedication
vi. Acknowledgement
viii. Foreword
xii. Review
xiv. Introduction

Chapter

1	A Call to Service	1
2	Deceptive Spirits	7
3	Fair is the Road that leads to Hell	15
4	The Wages of Sin	19
5	He came that we might live	25
6	For better or worse, not even in death do us part	31
7	Free at last	39
8	Chosen without a choice	49
9	Spiritual Warfare: How it began	53
10	Covered by theblood	67
11	Steps to Deliverance	77
12	Know Your Calling	87
13	Loose him and let him go	93
14	Strongholds	103
15	Identifying an unclean spirit	117
16	Conducting a deliverance	127
17	Spells and Curses	137
18	Curses in the Form of a Spell	151
19	Conclusion	165
	Testimonies	171

DEDICATION

First of all, I must give the highest thanks and praise to the Lord Jesus Christ for having created me. I must thank Him for His unconditional love and guidance. In addition, I would like to thank Him for bringing me out of the camp of darkness and into His marvellous Kingdom.

It is to Him, that I dedicate this book.

I also dedicate this book to my wonderful mother, Violet, whom I love so much. Without her what would I do?

To my daughters Kadian and Shadine and my niece Kerry-Ann.

To my sons Marlon, Junaid and Kevan and my grandson Javan.

To my wonderful husband Arthur and to Richard who has worked so hard in putting this book together.

To all my fellow workers at End Time Ministry. I thank you all for your encouragement and support.

VI

ACKNOWLEDGEMENT

I must give thanks to the Lord, for blessing me with some wonderful spiritual gifts, amongst which, is the gift of discernment.

I believe that every church leader should be able to look beyond the smiles and the beautiful outfits of the members of their assembly, and see the pain, hurt and baggage that is so often being carried by the people sitting in their pews.

There are times when I have been moved to tears as I counsel individuals that have come under the attack of the enemy. The burden of pain, hurt, and humiliation that they carry is often difficult to comprehend. Their self-esteem and self-confidence can be so badly damaged that it is truly only the Lord that can restore them.

If only we as Christians could clearly see the deep burning wounds embedded in some of these people. If we could only understand the kind of lies that satan tells them, or have insights into the strongholds that grip them when they visit us.

On speaking to such people, many will appear to be speaking for themselves. However, if we were able to truly discern, we would know that what is really speaking is the demon that has possessed the lives of those individuals; that it is he that is truly communicating with you as it looks at you through cold glassy eyes. When we consider these things, we have to ask ourselves some probing questions. How do we justify sitting back in our assemblies whilst allowing such wounded children to die without Christ?

When we view these spiritual problems in relation to the kingdom of God, St Matthew tells us that:

The Kingdom of God has been suffering violence from the beginning and that the violence takes it by force. ST MATTHEW 11:12

In the current spiritual dispensation, it is evident that God is raising up a set of militant spiritual warriors who are storming Hell s gates and who are taking God s kingdom by force. These warriors will not sit by and allow God's children to continue to be battered by satan and his legions of darkness.

We believe in holiness, and recognise that without holiness it is impossible to see God's face. At the same time, we are not too holy to trample on satan, his principalities, powers or the rulers of the darkness of this world.

We militantly take a stand for Jesus and continue to spiritually drive away every dark force from our churches and from the lives of God's children.

We stand on the word of God, sealed by his blood and dressed in righteousness and we zealously fight for the Kingdom of God.

As you read this book, may it be a blessing to your soul and may God so bless you that you too will stand for Him against the Kingdom of darkness.

FOREWORD

It is with great privilege that I am forwarding this book for Pastor Lona Copeland-Blake. As a man of God who has been personally involved in this great deliverance ministry, I am very proud of this work and I must say that I have learnt so much from this mighty woman of God.

Since I began ministering in End Time Ministry, less than a year prior to the writing of this book, I have seen more miracles than during my twenty prior years of walking with the Lord.

Within the Church of God of Prophecy where I am a minister, we have always stood for holiness, and I was certain that holiness alone was sufficient to fight against the powers of hell.

It was not until I began to share fellowship with End Time Ministry that I came to realise that it takes a militant spirit to take authority over these forces.

I never knew that someone could be cursed, through, for example, the placing of a curse on him or her, or that demons in the form of various creatures could inhabit the life of a person.

I now realise that there are many individuals who are silently suffering from these evil and malicious forces, and furthermore, that they do not care who they attack.

Nevertheless, God is now fulfilling the promises He made in Joel Chapter 2:28.

And it shall come to pass afterward that I will pour out my Spirit upon all flesh; and your sons and your daughters shall prophesy, your old men shall dream dreams, your young man shall see visions. JOEL 2:28

I can feel a mighty spiritual push in the spiritual realm, and I feel that the Lord is now moving His church into a new era; into a place where children of God will need to put on their gear for Holy war and stand up against the host of darkness.

I can now hear a holy war cry in Heaven, and in addition, I believe that God is speaking to the church today as He spoke to the church in Sardis:

I know thy works that thou art neither cold nor hot. I would that thou were cold or hot. So because thou art lukewarm and neither cold nor hot, I will spew you out of my mouth. REVELATION 3:15-16

I believe that God is now ready to take the church out of the comfort zone and into spiritual warfare. I have read several books on the topic of spiritual warfare but none is as thorough as I give you wings with which to fly .

I am quite impressed by the way in which the writer has been able to use her own experiences as the foundation for this work.

Pastor Copeland has not only explained the concept of spiritual warfare to the reader, but has also given examples, and in most cases I am able to bear witness with these.

As a minister of the gospel, Pastor Copeland s work has greatly challenged both my life, and my concepts on deliverance, and I am confident that as you read this book, it will do the same for you. I have walked into her meetings and have felt the presence of the Lord as the atmosphere has been charged with the presence of the Holy Ghost, and in those services, several miracles have taken place.

Throughout reading this book I sincerely hope that if you have not made the Lord your personal saviour, then you will do so. I pray that your souls will be richly blessed, and that whatsoever the devil has been using to bind you will be removed by the power of the Holy Ghost, and in the name of Jesus.

Pastor Lona Copeland-Blake is a schoolteacher, writer and Senior Pastor of End Time Ministry. This is the true story of a young woman who left her job as a schoolteacher to work as a media psychic. As her fame spread, she had people coming to see her from all over the world. She had invested large sums of money in business ventures and was doing very well for the kingdom of darkness.

Then God called her through ill health and as she said, even on broken pieces, I had to make it to the shore. She helplessly stood and watched as the Lord destroyed all that she had obtained, and then she humbled herself to the call of God and the Lord began to use her.

Pastor Copeland-Blake has a beautiful ministry of healing, deliverance, and prophesy. Her ministry is marked by the signs and wonders that followed the early churches.

Sick bodies have been healed, those that are in bondage have been set free, the demonised have been loosed, oppression has been lifted and most importantly, souls have been born for the kingdom of God. Her ministry is filled with the love of God and the anointing of the Holy Spirit.

She is loving and caring, but when it comes to the work of the Lord and the forces of darkness she is militant. Her church is victoriously and triumphantly warring against the forces of hell.

As she echoes the Holy war cry, she will tell you in a strong Jamaican accent:

Mi come wit blood in a mi eyes, and the sword of God in a mi hand.

Read on and be blessed by this powerful book.

Minister Herold Adams

REVIEW

I GIVE YOU WINGS WITH WHICH TO FLY

The title of this book alone engenders thoughts of freedom, peace and tranquillity. Haven t we all, at some time or other, wished we had wings that we could just spread like an eagle in order to fly away from the hopeless situations that we so often find ourselves in?

It is people who find themselves in these desperate situations who will most appreciate the teachings and lessons to be learned within the following pages.

This powerful book tells the story of one woman s journey from the world of sin, witchcraft, greed and occultism, through to, and beyond, her salvation through Christ Jesus.

Since entering her life, Jesus has transformed this lost and broken soul into a beautiful, powerful woman of God. Pastor Lona Copeland-Blake now stands fully armed with her experience of the kingdom of darkness and with authority through Christ Jesus. She marches boldly into the devil s territory and fearlessly claims back those whom are lost in the mire of life, and returns them to their rightful positions in the kingdom of God.

It is no wonder that the Father Himself named this book, that the message it speaks is one of deliverance, and what is certain to yield is hope and peace to the lost and the broken and to those whom have come under spiritual attack.

I pray that this book will bring peace to those in distress, hope to the unsaved, and guidance to those whom, like Pastor Copeland-Blake, have been called of God, to set the captives free.

Ruth Gordon

XIV
INTRODUCTION

To most believers, spiritual warfare is modern day theological language with which they are most unfamiliar. In particular, terms such as demons, devils, principalities, and powers, are often much feared expressions and many preachers would rather that such terminology were not used in their churches at all. There appears to be a phobia that such conversation might instigate the devil to let loose his horde of dark forces, and that somehow this might cause havoc in their peaceful assemblies.

On one occasion, I actually recall hearing a young minister telling his congregation categorically that there were no such things as demons. By making such unscriptural statements, what he was actually saying to his members was that the Bible is a book of myth and that although the text specifically refers to demons, there is actually no truth in those reports. Presumably Jesus must have cast something other than demons out of the Gaderene man, out of Jarius daughter, and out of the others whom he delivered. I also wonder what Jesus saw when He descended to hell to snatch the keys from satan.

I believe that any church that is not involved in spiritual warfare at this crucial time is in a fundamental dilemma, for satan the prince of this world has a work to do and his key objective is to ensure that churches fail. Any gathering of Christians is a threat to the kingdom of darkness and as such satan will do his utmost to prevent the growth of any assembly.

When we consider the many large opulent churches that have collapsed over night it is clear that this is often the result of the works of the forces of darkness. This is why Peter tells us that we must:

Be sober and vigilant because our Adversary the devil as a roaring lion walketh about seeking whom he may devour. 1 PETER 5:8

In this verse Peter is not speaking to sinners, but rather, he is directly addressing members of the body of Jesus Christ. Satan cannot be bothered with sinners; after all they belong to him already. His job is to hurt, defy and destroy those who preach or stand against him.

The role of the church on the other hand, is to declare redemption and salvation to sinners and to admonish against hell and eternal judgement. Given these distinct objectives, clearly satan will never disregard any blood washed militant church when it is the job of such churches to draw souls from the kingdom of darkness.

In the book of Ephesians, Paul explains that as Christians we are wrestling with the hosts of spiritual darkness. Once again Paul is addressing Christian members of a blood washed church in Ephesus and not the unsaved. Therefore, as saints of God we must be conscious that we are continually engaged in spiritual warfare.

We must recognise that spiritual warfare is not a weekly thing, that it is not a monthly battle, and neither is it a quarterly or yearly conflict. It is, in fact, a daily combat. This is why God has given us the armour and weaponry that should be used in battle to engage the enemy. If there were no battles then clearly there wouldn t be any need for the armour that God has scripturally provided us with.

It is also important to note that soldiers do not get dressed in their battle armour all of the time, and that when they are relaxing they wear ordinary attire. However, the prudent soldier is always alert so that in time of war he can pick up his weapons, put on his armour and prepare to fight. There is little value in soldiers going to the battlefront looking pretty, but with no weapons to defend themselves or to use to overcome the enemy.
Moreover, although armour is designed for use in the combat zone, this armour alone cannot prevent them from being injured. The actual power they must use to attack the enemy lies in their weapons. When the war cry echoes and guerrilla bombs begin to drop, gunshot begins to fire and arrows begin to soar, each soldier had better be ready for war. If they make the mistake of being unprepared, not only will they be defenceless, but they will also be left to the mercies of their opponents. In this situation their only hope would be a quick death.

ONLY AN UNPREPARED SOLDIER GOES INTO BATTLE UNARMED

Clearly, if there were no spiritual warfare, there would be no reason for us to be spiritually dressed. As such, any child of God who does not carry his ammunition with him should take some time to reflect upon his Christian lifestyle. If he is not fully armed he is obviously not ready to engage the enemy. He is exposed and consequently will be as grape under the feet of the foe.

However, with his armour in place he is more than a conqueror. What a beautiful and powerful thought, to know that with our ammunition in place, we are not just a conquering force but more than, above, and greater than conquerors! That s a wonderful assurance. Glory be to God!

Spiritual warfare has existed since the beginning of creation. When God cast the serpent from the Garden of Eden, He was engaged in spiritual warfare. I believe that one of the greatest spiritual battles to be fought on earth has to be that which was fought between Gideon and the Midianites, Amalekites and other children of the East.

The opposing groups had mighty armies and had recently defeated the Israelites. They were very proud of their recent victory, and in the ensuing battle, must have intended to completely exterminate the Israelites. However God saw their haughtiness and through their defeat in that battle he taught them a lesson that they would never forget.

The Bible shows us that Gideon initially had 32,000 men prepared for war, but that God thinned down his army to a mere 300. However, the Lord did not even allow those whom he had selected to fight; instead, all that he asked Gideon do was to blow the trumpet when the men gathered for war. The next image we see is that of the opponents killing each other.

There are many examples of spiritual battles found in the Bible. Among them are the battles of Jehosaphat where he and his few men fought various armies, all of whom were destroyed. We also see David, who was engaged in spiritual warfare with the giant Goliath, and also Joshua in the conquering of Jericho. This demonstrates that although the term spiritual warfare may be appear to be a current terminology for the body of Jesus Christ, it is certainly not a new activity, as it has been with us from the beginning of time.

One of the greatest spiritual battles ever fought must have been that which took place in the heavens in the anti-chaotic period. During this period a battle ensued between the Lord and Lucifer, who, with his rebellious angels, was cast from the presence of God and into the heavenlies.

This period must mark the beginning of all spiritual battles. Had there been no satan to battle against, there would be no need for spiritual conflict.

The Bible describes him as the fairest of angels , and states that he was so proud and so confident in himself that he desired to exalt himself above God. In fact, he began to feel that he was more important than God the Creator, and in the book of Ezekiel 28:15, he says that he desired to:

 Set himself above God.

We cannot imagine the magnitude of the spiritual conflict that took place in the heavens at that time, but we do know that as a result of the battle the Lord cast out satan and also about a third of his angels who had rebelled with him.

These rebellious angels are the same principalities, powers, and rulers of the darkness of this world of whom Paul speaks. They are still running wild on the earth and it is they whom Paul identifies as our opponents. In addition, Paul places these rulers in hierarchical order in the book of Ephesians chapter six. In the course of this text we will review their mode of operation, examine why they are so powerful and identify how we can be more than a match for them.

I believe that an effective deliverance minister would be one who has had a personal encounter with spiritual wickedness and would have actual experience of the kingdom of darkness. S/he would have studied the ways of the wicked one, and would have personally experienced some form of deliverance.

As a deliverance minister, and someone who has experienced all of the above, I am now writing this book from my own personal experience. As such this book details my involvement with the kingdom of darkness and records the experience that I have gained not only through my own deliverance, but also from the testimonies of many poor demonised individuals whom God is now using me to deliver.

When I was in the world, I could easily have been ranked among Britain s leading psychics. I was not just an under cover, low-keyed operator; in the realm of the psychics I was actually famous. For many years satan bestowed false honour upon me so as to keep me hooked to wealth, fame and the things of this world.

During this time I made television appearances, was featured on talk shows on many radio stations, and I had big write ups in national papers. People were visiting me for psychic help from all walks of life. I was wealthy, and I was making big money. In retrospect, I would say that I was, in fact, one of the biggest con artists in town.

This all changed, however, one wonderful day when Jesus came into my life, and He made all the difference. Nevertheless, before he came to save me from satan s grip I believe that He sent His angels to prepare the way, and what did he have them do?

He made sure that all the wealth that I had acquired from the kingdom of darkness was depleted. Furthermore, by the time the Lord really came for me, I was so sick that I was literally at the point of death; there was no money, no wealth, and no fame. I had nothing left to hang on to. The Lord stripped me of everything and then with outstretched arms, He gently drew me close to Him and called me into ministry. All that I came to the Lord with was a broken spirit and a hope of eternal life.

I thank God that now He has not only given me a wonderful husband, but also a church with many spiritual babies. We are on our way to glory and as the song says, we really feel like travelling on .

I was once a chicken with small wings and little feathers. Now God has transformed me into an eagle and He has given me wings with which to fly.

On coming to Jesus there were times when I had to fight for my life and I am certain that there were moments when the devil felt that I was completely defeated. He must have felt that I was finished and that there was no hope for me.

I can envisage the basement party that satan and his demons had prepared to celebrate my downfall. However, just when they believed that I was ready to die, in my spirit I saw the Lord stepped in like a mighty rush of wind and turned his party table over. Glory be to God, He has set this captive free.

Thank God I m free at last. I am no more in chains but by God s grace I am now part of the battle as it continues, because there are so many others who, just as I was bound, are also caught in satan s dirty Web and are being fooled by his counterfeit offers. Now I have the real thing and I thank God that it is available to all. It s wonderful, it s delightful, it s breathtaking, it s superb, it s everlasting and God s plan is for us to share it with others.

On the last occasion that the evil one tried to take my life, my doctor did her outmost to help me, but her medical solutions were unable to either diagnose or cure a spiritual problem. Her medical degree left her ill equipped to fight with principalities and powers. As such, when she witnessed my full recovery, she just could not understand it because it did not make physical sense. In total bewilderment I recall her asking me:

Is that Lona?

Yes doctor, it s me. I replied.

How did you do it? she asked, amazed.

Doctor! I explained excitedly. I know a man who can! Whenever you have patients who have the problems I had, then send them to me, because I know a man who can!

This is my testimony, which I hope will bring comfort and hope to all who have experienced or are experiencing any form of spiritual attack. God in his mercy did not only heal me, but He also invested the power in me to heal others and to cast demons out of those that are oppressed, in Jesus name. I thank God that he could now use me to deliver those who are under attack and that souls are also being saved for His kingdom. Read on and hear all about it.

Chapter 1

A Call to Service

'And the Lord called Samuel and he answered, 'here I am' And he ran to Eli and said 'here am I for thou calledst me' And he said 'I called not, lie down again' And he went and lay down.'
1 Samuel 3:4-5

HEARING AND RESPONDING TO THE CALL OF GOD

I was about twelve years old when the Lord first called me. Perhaps if I had a wise man to instruct me, as Samuel had Eli to instruct him, I would have known how to respond to the call of God, but as it happened I did not recognise his call and so I did not respond. I believe that if as a young child I had answered that first call of God, I would not have ventured down the demonic path that lay ahead of me.

The Lord gave me a vision in which I saw Him walking on the clouds towards me. Although I tried to run, I found that my legs were far too heavy to take me. I was so petrified, that I didn t know what do. I saw crowds of people watching me as I tried to run but I couldn t go very far.

As the Lord gently stretched His hands out towards me, I woke out of my sleep. In my childish fearfulness, I misinterpreted the vision to mean that I was about to die and that I had only escaped death because I was able to wake from my sleep.

When God gave me that vision I am certain that satan was lurking around me, very much aware that the Lord was calling me, and observing as the Lord tried to reach out to me. He must have realised even then, that if he could get to me before the Lord could, he would be able to use me for his demonic intentions and prevent me from stepping into that which God had purposed for my life.

Don t be fooled into believing that satan does not know every child of God who has a calling upon his life. In truth it is his earnest desire to get to that individual before God can. I can almost hear him in his eerie voice saying, If I can get that one then I could do a lot of damage with her.

This was confirmed one day at a deliverance service that I attended before I began my ministry. During the service a demon-possessed woman was being delivered and I heard the demon speaking through that young lady. The voice was that of a man and he spoke plainly.

You are a strong man I could exchange this girl's spirit with that of yours If I could get your spirit then I would do a lot of things with it.

It was as if satan himself was speaking. We must all be aware that Lucifer is able to identify any good strong spirit that can build the kingdom of God and do harm to the kingdom of darkness, and his aim is simply to get to those spirits first.

Many people, myself included, suffer at the hands of satan purely because when God calls us we do not answer.

Sometimes the Lord calls us to protect us from the danger that lies ahead of us, danger that we are often incapable of seeing or anticipating. So many times we could have avoided some of those terrible ordeals that we have endured if we had only responded to His first call.

SPIRITUAL GUIDANCE AND LEADERSHIP

The prophet Hosea tells us that:

My people are destroyed for lack of knowledge. HOSEA 3:6

In some cases people do not answer the call because they are unable to distinguish between the voice of the Lord and that of the evil one. Moreover, even if some are able to hear His voice, they often have difficulty finding a good spiritual leader who can guide and mentor them, or who can help them with their spiritual walk.

The sad fact is that many churches have moved from the fundamentals of the Christian faith and are failing to recognise the instruction of the Lord as explained in the book of Matthew.

And He called His twelve disciples together, and gave them power and authority over all devils and to cure diseases. And He sent them to preach the kingdom of God and to heal the sick. LUKE 9:1-2

Instead of focusing on the biblical principles of activating power and authority over all evils and curing disease, many pastors seem to have misdirected their attentions into doing what Burger King, Kentucky and MacDonald's have done. They want to make a name for themselves.

It is because of this problem that many souls that are destined for the kingdom of heaven are lost in this merchandised spiritual market. They have no one to counsel them, no one to lead them, no clear path to follow and consequently they are lost.

There is a danger that we have let the marketing of the gospel overshadow the true beauty of good Christian living and the glory of God Almighty.

There are many broken souls in some of our churches, some of which are badly in need of some form of counselling from the pastors in whom they have placed their trust and confidence. Instead of having easy access to these pastors, Pastors are often so busy that individuals can sometimes find themselves on a waiting list for up to a year to get an opportunity to see them.

As pastors it is our responsibility to ensure that knowledge and guidance is available to those who need them. We must ensure that we have anointed ministers in our midst who are ordained by God, and available to counsel and advise those who are in need of guidance.

Furthermore, Pastors need to let God be God and allow Him to select the people He wishes to anoint. The anointing that each individual receives from the Holy Spirit is unique, and moreover, whatever anointing God gives to a leader can only be used by that person for the Kingdom of God, and for the time in which it is given.

Yes, we can pass on the mantle, but God Himself must hand pick those members onto whom we must pass the anointing. In addition, the anointing is provided along with the gifts of the spirit as Paul describes to us in the book of second Corinthians.

Now there are diversities of gifts but the same spirit. And there are differences of operation but the same God which worketh all in all. 2 COR.12: 1-3

As such, one person might have the gift of healing while another might have the gift of prophecy, or it is possible that an individual may have all of the spiritual gifts. What it does not mean, however, is that because gifts are operative in the churches that we as leaders should become too money orientated, self-centred and egotistical, that we should have no time for the broken souls in our assemblies.

God is depending on us to minister to the sheep that He sends to our pastures. In addition, we cannot assume that others will care for our flocks in the same way that we do. When we leave our flocks for too long with our select groups we need to be very certain that we are not leaving them to the mercies of wolves.

It is not surprising that so many little churches are formed from larger ones without the consent of the senior pastors. The Bible tells us that we often have wolves in our midst, who we unconsciously train and instruct, only to later observe them stealing our sheep.

Beware of false prophets who come to you in sheep s clothing but inwardly they are ravening wolves. MATTHEW 7:15

These wolves will rip our assemblies to pieces as soon as they are given the opportunity to do so.

In addition, Pastors cannot always depend on their ministerial board to carry out their pastoral responsibilities. Ultimately the Pastor is the feeder of the sheep in his flock.

One Sunday not long ago a young girl came into one of our meetings on crutches. As it happened, on that particular Sunday I was feeling unwell, and as such when the anointing fell in the church, I called on a few members to pray with her.

I watched as the members prayed and prayed for the girl but could see that nothing was happening. As I stood there looking on, the Lord spoke to me.
 Lona, He said. My glory I will give to no man, and what I give to you is not for you to give to anyone else. You cannot just send someone to do what you are supposed to do. Go and anoint the young girl.

Although I was feeling quite unwell I walked over to her, and asked someone to stand behind her. As I touched her she fell to the floor. The Lord then told me to leave her lying there, because He was performing a spiritual operation on her. The girl drifted into a spiritual sleep and when she woke up, she was walking. Within one week she had made a complete recovery.

God is looking for leaders who can take care of sheep and those who can really lead souls to Calvary. He is searching for those who know His voice, and those who will not try to be God, who like wolves will desire to steal the glory from Him.

Eli, Samuel s mentor, was such a man. When the Lord called Samuel, in first Samuel chapter three, Samuel did not recognise the voice of God. Samuel was not only very young in years; he was also spiritually immature. He had not heard the Lord speak before, and therefore he was not acquainted with His voice. Samuel believed that he had heard the voice of his spiritual leader and so he ran to him.

On realising that it was in fact the Lord who was calling Samuel, Eli told him exactly how he should respond:

Go lie down and it shall be if He call thee that thou shalt say, speak Lord, thy servant heareth. 2 SAMUEL 2: 9

It is essential that we have strong spiritual leaders like Eli, just as it is essential that we learn to recognise the voice of God.

THE DANGER OF A REPROBATE MIND

As a child I foolishly believed that I was too young to answer when the Lord called me. I now realise that if the Lord did not believe that there was a work for me to do, even at that tender age, then He would not have called me. Samuel himself was only twelve years when the Lord called him.

The day after the Lord gave me that vision I was so paranoid that I did not know what to do. I had quite a good relationship with my mother and usually felt that I could talk to her, but for some reason this time I did not feel that I could tell her what was happening to me.

I spent days under conviction, but never shared my burden with anyone. As far as I was concerned, I didn t need anyone to tell me that there was a God. I had seen Him for myself and because of my misunderstanding I suffered in silence and cried for days. As time went by the crying began to cease, but I then began to have all kinds of weird dreams, and in my ignorance and naivety, I still did not give my heart to God.

Sometimes when the Lord calls us and we do not respond to his voice, He will leave us to our reprobate minds . Paul tells us this in the book of Romans:

And even as they did not like to retain God in their knowledge, God gave them over to their reprobate mind to do the things which are not convenient. ROMANS. 1:28

The Greek word being used here for reprobate is adokimos, meaning in this context, rejected or and cast away . The Greek word for convenient is, kathelon, which means fit or proper .

5

Paul is warning us that when we reject the Lord, He will leave us to do the things that are improper and unsuitable. He is telling us that our thoughts will continue to be filthy, and that as a result we will pursue the ways of evil and do things that are immoral and distasteful. Many people have turned their backs on God and allowed their reprobate minds to rule their lives.

Having turned my back on the Lord, His presence subsequently departed from my life and I fell into sin. The devil then saw the opportunity to come in and so he did.

Several years later, I awoke one morning to hear an audible voice telling me that I had the ability to do psychic reading and that I should pursue this. The voice told me that I could earn large sums of money and that I would acquire substantial materialistic wealth through using this ability.

Without God in my life my mind was unprotected from the attacks of the enemy. Just as God was able to communicate with me spiritually, so too was the enemy, and as Paul had warned, my reprobate mind was now open to pursue the things of evil. The day that I chose to listen to this voice instead of the voice of the Lord marked a tragic turning point in my life.

Chapter 2

Deceptive Spirits

Then said Saul to his servants, seek me a woman that with a familiar spirit that I may go and enquire of her. And his servants said to him, behold there is a woman that hath a familiar spirit at Ednor. And the woman said unto him, behold thou knowest what Saul hath done, how he hath cut off those that have familiar spirits, and the wizards out of the land wherefore then layest thou a snare for my life. 1Samuel 1:8 –9

THE VOICE OF THE ENEMY

The last thing that I had expected to happen to me was to have some unknown voices telling me what I should do with my life. However the most important news of all was to be told that I would be making a lot of money. My desire to have material wealth was one of the things that nearly cost me my life.

The devil is well aware of human weaknesses and of our desire to excel materially. As such lust for material wealth is a frequent deception used by the enemy to lead many away from the paths of righteousness. It is so sad to know that even folks who claim to be blood washed, tongue talking, feet stamping children of God are being conned by the evil one who so easily leads them astray with this spirit of deception and greed.

After hearing this deception from the evil one, I became so excited that I immediately ran to a friend to break what I had perceived as being good news to her. You see as far as I was concerned I had discovered that I had a powerful gift. However, rather than good news, in truth all that I had received was a curse.

Satan had realised that God was about to bestow His wonderful gifts upon my life, and in my ignorance he had succeeded in tapping into my weakness to tempt me and redirect my path away from the things of God. He was able to endow me with an evil spiritual substitute, a counterfeit of God s awesome Holy Spirit and heavenly gifts. What satan gave me, was a familiar spirit.

FAMILIAR SPIRIT

A familiar spirit is any unclean spirit that speaks through or to a person and can be used to perform fortune telling or divination.

As children of God, we must be careful not to transit from church to church without having the blessings of our pastors or church leaders. There are so many evil spirits around today that are deceiving God s children. The Bible tells us that we must test the spirit , and it is this that many Christians are failing to do. Testing the spirit means ensuring that the spirit we are dealing with is of God and not of the devil.

Beloved believe not every spirit, but try the spirits whether they are of God: because many false prophets are gone out into the world. 1 John 4:1

The Bible tells us that in these last days there will be many false prophets. These deceivers travel around filled with familiar spirits and are preaching in the name of Jesus.

To these iniquitous individuals, the preaching of the gospel has become big business. It is not about spreading the word of God, but rather it is about empire building and self-gratification. Frequently these ungodly desires are underpinned by practices that relate directly to the appeasement of false gods and idols.

For example, many Christians are aware of the many questionable gifts and powers that have emerged from remote places in Africa and Asia. In many of these examples we are told of individuals venturing into the hills and undergoing truly dreadful and painful rituals in order to obtain power that effectively allows them to do evil.

According to the pacts that are made with the devil, this power will only last for seven years after which the individual will lose it. In return for these gifts they form churches, which bring the individual the wealth, and authority they desire, while adding to the devil s kingdom by luring innocent believers out of the presence of God.

Given this background it is not surprising that so many churches are springing up calling themselves deliverance ministries at this time, but as time goes by we find that they are, here today, gone tomorrow .

In some cases these false prophets are very eloquent and outspoken about their great deliverance ministries, but when you participate in these services, you cannot feel any anointing within them. Oh, to see some of these ministers on the television telling all sorts of lies! They are as dry as parched corn. In their futile endeavours to steal the glory from God, they use all manner of deception and lies to perform their so-called miracles. In fact, they often pretend to be healers just like the anointed Benny Hinn.

You will not be surprised then when shortly after watching one of these fake performances you switch on your television to find that their shows are n longer on air because they were not operating under the anointing. Then you begin to read all about their scandalous behaviour in the national papers.

It was only about a year to the time of writing this book that I heard of a most powerful pastor who had a wonderful prosperity anointing. In fact, the anointing was so great that small churches had closed down and had joined up with him to get some of the prosperity that was flowing from the pulpit to the pew.

I was told about this great man of God who was prospering so much that he had bought his own aeroplane in a short space of time, and who had his own aeroplane bay. He was giving millions of pounds to the poorer members of his congregation and, of course, he was going the Bible way because he was making sure that widows were properly cared for which is a scriptural responsibility as the Bible says that we should care for the widows.

A friend of mine invited me to attend one of his meetings and when we arrived, we discovered that the gathering was tremendous. He had an arena, which we were all told belonged to the church, and we were informed that the church members had contributed thousands of pounds towards the purchase of this building.

The first thing that I noticed was that he was not a preacher. He began his sermon by bragging about the millions that he had. He told the congregation that when his money went into the bank it had devalued the pound, because it was so much.

He called a young lady, whom he claimed had once been a witch and she testified that when she had come to him he had cast the witchcraft demon out of her. He proceeded to explain that the Holy spirit had told him to give her a million pounds and that it would be deposited in the bank for her.

With the gift of discernment I was able to swiftly recognise that the spirits I was observing were not of God. It grieved my spirit to observe so many innocent Children of God being misled by this demon masquerading as a child of God.
I walked out of that church that day, feeling completely lost and empty. I was really sorry for those people who most obviously believed the lies of this conman.

I tried to tell my friend that the man was a counterfeit, a false prophet. I tried to explain that the preacher was possessed by a demon spirit, but she just would not listen to me. As far as she was concerned, many people were getting their blessings there and she was not going to miss out on hers.

Shortly after that, someone brought me a Christian magazine. This preacher s picture was on the front page and his story filled the paper. The headline read,

In The Name Of Money!

People did not attend that church for their salvation, neither did the pastor preach in the name of Jesus. Everything was done in the name of money.

These are the types of occultists into whom satan is placing his counterfeit familiar spirits. Moreover, he is sending them as undercover agents to do damage to the kingdom of heaven. Fortunately, their glory is always short-lived because it is bogus, and despite the devil s efforts, the true glory of Jesus can never fade. Not only is it permanent but also it will shine brighter and brighter as the believer sinks deeper and deeper in the Lord.

Among the many horrible things that later became known, was the awful confirmation that this bogus pastor had not even purchased the arena, but had kept over a million pounds of the church payers contributions. On the last report we had of him, he was looking for an escape route to leave the country.

You see our intentions, and our heart s desires, must be clean. It was Saul himself who destroyed all of the familiar spirits and idol worship out of Israel, and yet when the Spirit of the Lord departed from him, the first thing he did was to go in search of one of those same spirits.

People that have familiar spirits are on direct assignments from hell. In the case of clairvoyants, witches and readers who actually try to call up dead spirits, the devil in his trickery provides them with a substitute spirit that resembles that of the spirit that the seeker desired to consult.

People are easily deceived by such spirits, and after one of these sessions will go away thinking that they have really just seen their dead mother or grandfather. What they have done in fact is consulted with a lying evil spirit, and that spirit has deceived them.

During Saul s encounter with the familiar spirit, the woman he visited asked him whom he wished to speak to. The bible says she asked him:

Whom shall I bring up unto thee? And he said bring me up Samuel.
1 SAMUEL 28:11

This woman must have known Samuel, and as she was accustomed to calling up the dead, she really should not have been surprised when Samuel appeared. Her evident surprise therefore, was solely because she was accustomed to calling up imitation spirits and as such she had expected a counterfeit to appear. When the Lord sent the real spirit of Samuel to teach Saul a lesson, she was alarmed. In her horror she demonstrated once again that she did not know that the real spirit of Samuel would have appeared in the next verse:

And when the woman saw Samuel she cried with a loud voice. And the woman spake to Saul saying Why hast thou deceived me for thou art Saul 1 Samuel 28:12

As a result of his consultation with familiar spirits, Samuel tells Saul the dreaded news that he, Saul, was going to die the next day.

A blood washed child of God cannot listen to lying familiar spirits. I have observed that as soon as a prophet comes to town under the umbrella of Christianity, Christians will run to him to get a prophetic word.

The inherent problem is that many of these prophets are in fact transporting a lying familiar spirit with them. It is crucial therefore, that as children of God, we test the spirit at all times. If we do not know how to test the spirit, then we should lock in and pray to God. He is our problem solver; he is our burden bearer. He knows the desire of our hearts and He has the answer.

Although we may not know, we can be certain that He always knows counterfeit. Let us be prudent and cautious and not be in too much of a hurry. If you trust in God to supply all of your needs and to take care of all your problems, then there is really no need to rush. Isaiah reiterates this in the following verse:

Therefore thus saith the Lord, behold I lay in Zion for a foundation, a stone a tried stone, a precious corner stone, a sure foundation: He that believeth shall not make haste. Isaiah 28:16.

God is our sure foundation and when we submit our ways to Him and trust in him, then we can avoid receiving any false teaching from a prophet that comes to speak to us.

AGREEING WITH THE ENEMY

When we do receive from that familiar spirit, we place ourselves in a rather peculiar situation. By accepting what they are saying to us, we actually join in implicit agreement with them and this can cause this spirit to hang around us. The last thing that we want in our Christian walk is a dirty, foul spirit connecting itself to us.

The Holy Spirit is not a counterfeit. He s a clean Spirit, a true Spirit, a pure Spirit, a kind spirit, a comfortable Spirit, and a healing Spirit. He is reliable and we can depend on him. As such, the last thing we need is to enter into any agreement with the devil.

You do not have to knowingly enter into a covenant with the evil one. Once he sees an opportunity to inhabit your life, or a doorway through which he can enter, then he is going to do so.

There are two types of pact or covenant that one can enter into with satan. The first is an agreeable contract. In this instance you may knowingly and voluntarily have entered into this arrangement, or you may have been forced into the agreement with him. The contract is one that has been made with full knowledge of the parties to the contract.

You would therefore make an explicit agreement with the devil to serve him and to do his bidding and you would probably have to go through some kind of ritual or initiation. (For more information on pact and covenant with the devil, I would strongly recommend the book, He Came to Set the Captive Free. by Doctor Rebecca Brown.)

For others like me, the agreement that was set in place was implicit. One day I was a schoolteacher, the next I was a psychic reader. I made no agreement with satan, nor was I formerly involved in any occultic practice. I later discovered, however, that there was a generational curse of familiar spirits in my family ties. Therefore, although I did not enter into any agreement with the devil, a contractual agreement had been formed with my past generations, either by a contract of agreement or by someone placing a curse on my family. This curse would have been passed down my family line.

The Hebrew word for familiar spirit is owb. This is translated as a mumble as from a water skin because of its hollow sound, a bottle, a necrometer, or a ventriloquist. It is also used to refer to demon spirits that possess mediums and means to imitate dead human beings, make predictions, promote doctrines etc.

If you have a keen interest in New Age thinking, tarot cards, ougo board, swinging the pendulum, astrology, tea reading, card reading, hi Chung, candle burning, incense, oils, herbs and washes to name a few, then be ye warned, you are in danger, and you are playing with your life.

This is a very dangerous game to play and once you begin playing it, you can become hooked very quickly. You are indirectly and unconsciously making a covenant with satan, and once he enters through that doorway you will not be able to get him out without the Lord holding your hands. The devil is always on the look out for new recruits, and as soon as you begin to dabble with his spirits you are automatically placed on satan s list of recruits to become a witch, or to be used in his kingdom for his purposes.

The list of activities outlined above is occultic and as soon as you bring these things into your house you have opened your doors and let the devil in. Moreover, once he comes in, you will have great difficulty getting him out. He will not just leave of his own accord.

Let us take the tarot card as an example. On the face of each card is a picture, which symbolises some form of Greek occultic practice. The devil s demons are therefore associated with each of those cards and as soon as you pick them up and begin to use them, you will begin to draw demons to you.

These forces linger around actually looking for the opportunity to get into you. As soon as they are inside of you, you will find yourself with a false belief that may be similar to that which I had. You may find yourself believing that you are gifted, when, in fact, you are possessed with a spirit of divination.

In the book of Acts, the young girl had a familiar spirit of python.

And it came to pass that as we went to prayer, a certain damsel possessed with a spirit of divination met us which brought her master much gain by soothsaying. ACTS 16:16

The Greek translation describes the spirit of divination, which this girl possessed as a spirit of python or Apollo. According to fable, Pytho was a huge serpent that had an oracle on Mt. Parnassus, and was famous for predicting future events. It was believed that the spirit of Apollo Pythius influenced all mystics who pretended to foretell events. It is said that people under the influence of this demon would physically swell up and speak and behave in a frenzied state.

The devil really knows man s weaknesses and he is aware that man will always seek to find out things about the past, present, and future. Satan s use of mystics is just another of his schemes to draw God s children to him and keep them out of God s presence. Notice, however, that Paul was able to quickly identify this evil spirit. It is almost amusing that the spirit tries to hide its identity from Paul, and speaking through the young girl it says boldly:

These men are the servants of the most high God, which show unto us the way to salvation. ACTS 16:17

WHEN THE DEVIL SPEAKS THE TRUTH

 satan has a way of speaking the truth to deceive us. Certainly the spirit was speaking the truth. This declaration was, however, simply a trick of the devil and an endeavour to discredit the message of the Apostles. He wanted the people to think that the Apostles were in league with the demon spirits, who were telling these lies through the demon-possessed medium.

Nonetheless, Paul was not deceived by the trick and he took authority over the demons and cast them out in the name of Jesus. Familiar spirits are no match for a blood washed child of God.

During one of my Bible lectures, a young lady was calmly sitting in our midst that was possessed with a familiar spirit. It was a rather Holy Ghost power packed evening. Suddenly, I heard this voice coming from the woman that was not her own and was more like that of a male. You had better take this serious you know! This is not a joke thing! It shouted. This is serious business!

One of our evangelists quickly identified the spirit and began to aggressively take authority over it. Immediately, God gave me a word of knowledge that we could not deal aggressively with that spirit, otherwise the young lady would become fearful and would run away. We were able to use wisdom and cast out those demons.

Evil spirits can be no match for a blood washed child of God because we are equipped with the Holy Spirit who can discern every trick and deception of the enemy. What is clear from our deliverance ministry, however, is that evil spirits can conceal themselves in all kinds of people, and often the most innocent looking individuals can be carrying the most terrible demons. Only the Holy Spirit himself can root up these evils and equip us with the wisdom that we need to deliver those who are suffering from demon possession.

Chapter 3

Fair is the road
that leads to Hell

'And seek not ye what ye shall eat or what ye shall drink, neither be ye of doubtful mind. For all these things do the nations of the world seek after and your father knoweth that you have need of these things. But rather seek ye the kingdom of God and all these things will be added unto you' Luke 12: 19

DOUBLE MINDEDNESS

The Greek word for the phrase doubtful mind above is meteorize. This means to raise in mid air, suspend, fluctuate, to be anxious or to be carried about as meteors which are moved about with the currents, tossed up and down between hope and fear . In the previous scripture, the Lord is rebuking the heathen who superstitiously seek guidance by consulting witches, magicians, meteors, astrologers and all sorts of occultists.

A person with a settled mind will not consult a witch. It is due to double mindedness or a mind, which is being tossed, and driven as described above, that one goes in search of answers from such satanic people. The information that you receive from these witches is usually so unsettled, dubious and incomplete that you are forced to go back to them for further clarification. In so doing, you are become dependent on them and the misinformation that they provide you with.

In fact, when you begin to dabble and to see fortune-tellers you will actually acquire a spirit of occultism and it is this spirit, which will keep pulling you back to them. It is commonly our lust for earthly pleasures, coupled with our inability to wait upon the Lord that leads us to these sorts of people.

This lustfulness is generally our greatest downfall in life. The Bible is clearly telling us in Luke 12:19 that our need for the necessities of life should take second place in our lives as we seek first God s Kingdom and His righteousness.

Unfortunately God is not given any place in the lives of many people. As long as they can live in a nice comfortable house, drive a nice car, have a decent job and can afford to splash out on earthly, materialistic pleasures, then as far as they are concerned, they are living a fulfilled life.

I give thanks to the Lord for allowing me to be introduced to the pleasures of the world, and for allowing me to realise that I could have died and left all of those things behind, to be destined for a life of everlasting torment. I have been to several funerals and to date I have never seen anyone being buried with earthly luxuries that they can take with them. No matter how much they have acquired in this world, they must step into the next life without them.

On discovering that I had the ability to perform psychic reading, I immediately began to think of all the earthly gains that I could acquire and in no time my house was packed with people coming to me for readings . These people came from all over the world, and even when I was on vacation abroad, clients from England would have called their relatives abroad who would to come and visit me during my vacation. I was quickly becoming famous, and with the fame came the money.

My notoriety began to spread and soon I had journalists at my door asking for interviews. Within a short while I became a media psychic, which meant that I had the rich and famous coming to see me from all walks of life. As these celebrities came, so did the fortune. I realised that these people did not care whether you were lying or not, as long as you told them what they wanted to hear. Money was not a problem for them and as such they would pay large sums for what they perceived to be solid information.

In retrospect I feel nothing for those people except complete sorrow, because I now know that they are still in satan s slave market. He has conned them into believing and accepting lies, and into living lives that are completely false. For most of them, their sole desire is to remain in the limelight. Sadly, many of them have such a tragic end. As soon as satan is finished with them, he usually drives them into insanity, drugs or death.

While many of these stars portray a life of complete ease and total satisfaction, some are in fact going around with twisted minds. They are sometimes very confused, and although they appear to have so much, they actually have so little. They are often carrying spirits of greed, which drive them to seek for more and more, and push them deeper into insanity.

THE PROBLEM WITH THE QUICK FIX

As time went by I found that this is precisely what occurred in my life. The more things I obtained, the more that I desired.

As a simple example you might begin by not being able to drive a car. You then find yourself driving a little car of the oldest model. As time goes by that car is no longer good enough for you, so you begin to work towards buying a better car. When you finally get your new car it is the latest model and design and it is all that you had desired initially. However you will still continue to seek for a more luxurious type. In fact luxury alone is now insufficient, and what you now desire must be so unique that it is one of a kind.

I am not by any means saying that we shouldn t seek to have the best in life, God clearly desires the best for his children. However the scripture also tells us that the reason there is so much sin in the world, through occultism, drug abuse, sexual perversion, fraud theft and so forth is because:

The god of this world hath blinded the minds of them, which believe not. Lest the light of the glorious gospel of Christ who is the image of God should shine unto them. 2 CORINTHIANS. 4:4

These folks believe so much in this quick fix that satan offers them that it is generally quite difficult for them to realise when they are being set up for a fall. It is therefore no surprise that by the time they would have come to this realisation that they would have completely fallen. And some of them never get the chance to pick themselves up again, because as soon as satan is finished with them, his only intention is to kill them.

He encourages them to store up all these earthly treasures, ensuring that they are making no preparation for their souls. They have no hope for everlasting life. However, Peter tells us that as Christians:

We are begotten into a lively hope by the resurrection of Jesus Christ from the dead, to an inheritance, incorruptible and undefiled and that fadeth not away, reserved in heaven for us. 1 PETER 1:4

What an assurance, to know that we may not be earthly stars, but we are redeemed by the blood of Jesus and have now become:

a chosen generation, a royal priesthood, a holy nation, a peculiar people. 1 PETER 2:9.

Satan may be offering earthly glamour to this world, but it is only when the Lord comes to take over rulership that everyone will know who the real stars are. We are confident that although we may suffer just as the Apostle Paul suffered in this

life, we have a hope of being with Christ forever. Paul tells us that:
We are troubled on every side, yet not distressed, we are perplexed but not despair, persecuted, but not forsaken, cast down but not destroyed
2 Corinthians. 4:8-9.

Further on in the same passage he says that:

We look not at the things which are seen, but at the things which are not seen for the things which are seen are temporal, but the things which are not seen are eternal. 2 Corinthians 4:18

By now my priority was to be rich and famous. As a result greed set in and I began to care less and less about how much I was charging for my services. People knew that I was famous and they wanted to hear from a famous psychic. As far as I was concerned they had to pay to hear from me.

My home was like a shrine with all sorts of psychic tools on which the enemy had me hooked. I used to pray at that time but I was unable to do so without having candles burning at the same time. I always had to rely on oil, incense and other demonic attractions in my futile endeavours to speak to the Lord. I had no idea that these utensils actually drew more demons towards me and took me further away from presence of God.

People were coming to me for a quick fix to solve their problems and the devil was happy to use me to provide demonic solutions. Those who came were trapped in sin, just as I was trapped in it, in my endeavour to help them. There was no offer of salvation and no offer of eternal life. All that was offered was a temporary solution to a more serious problem than I even understood. Without God there was no solution to the problems that these people had. All that they succeeded in doing was to draw themselves deeper into sin.

Chapter 4

The Wages of Sin

And Saul's servants said unto him, behold now, an evil spirit from God troubleth thee. 1 Samuel 16:15

THE MEANING OF AN EVIL SPIRIT

To understand the meaning of the phrase evil spirit, it would be best to analyse each word individually.

The Greek word for evil in this context is **Poneros**. This means bad, worthless, causing pain, and sorrow. It is the same word that is used to describe the seven bad spirits of Matthew 12:45.

In addition, this word is also used to describe the spirits in the man that Jesus cured in Luke 7:21 and those which Paul cast out of the people in Acts 19:12.

The Greek word for spirit is **Pneuma**, meaning immaterial, invisible, and powerful. An evil spirit is therefore something that is worthless, generally bad and powerful, and which causes pain. The Gadarene lunatic, out of whom Jesus drove the legions, had to be kept in chains because of the power or strength of those demons. The Bible says that:

Often times it had caught him, and he was kept bound with chains and in fetters. Luke 8:29

When the demons were controlling the lunatic boy of Matthew 17, The father said that the child:

...falleth into the fire and into the water. Matthew 17:17

On completion of this book I want you to understand how evil and dangerous these evil spirits are, and furthermore, how they can affect human beings and eventually destroy lives. It is really an awful thing to step out of the presence of the Lord and to be taken over by such unclean forces.

I was enjoying my fame and was sinking so much deeper into the works of the enemy that I had little interest in anything else except money. The more I had, the more that I wanted. I am sure that there are Christian people reading this book who can identify with this, and if so it is possible that you have a stronghold of greed in your life that you need to deal with. We will discuss strongholds in more depth later in the book.

I was not aware that the Lord had His eyes on me and that He was only allowing me to fall on my own swords .

It all began one Halloween night, a night which is probably the most dreadful of the year. This is the time when demons are let loose, and when satan has his dirty parties.

During this time all sorts of immoral things happen. Demons have sex with witches and satanic activities take place involving young children. In addition they indulge in intoxicating drinking to incite lurid sexual desires. For centuries, this has been marked as the time when they, satan s followers come together to do their incantations and to cast spells.

That day, I had just ended a long day of doing occultic work. I sent my niece to the shop and shortly after she had left, I heard my doorbell ring. Without looking through the peephole to see who was there, I opened the door and said, Come in! but to my surprise, there was no one there. I stepped outside and looked up and down the road, but saw no one. Confused, I shut the door, and told myself that it was only little children playing.

Shortly after this incident I began to feel ill. I was feeling so bad that I was only just about able to hold on until my niece returned. I actually felt that I was on the verge of death.

I did not go to the doctor but spent the next few days using all of the occultic paraphernalia that I had in the house to try and make myself better. I tried all sorts of things except the Lord Jesus. Although I felt a mild improvement, I was still very ill. All these tools did was enabled me to hang in there for a while.

Then one awful night, as I lay in bed I literally felt when a huge cat eased itself into my body. The following morning when I tried to get out of bed I was physically unable to. I was both vomiting and having diarrhoea simultaneously.

As I was unable to even make my way to the doctor s surgery, my doctor had to make a house call to visit me. Unfortunately, whatsoever he gave me had only made me worst. I felt a heavy oppression all around me and I doubt that I slept for more than a couple of hours that night.

The following day, I forced myself to take a cab to the surgery. The doctor looked at me and said:

Lona, I will not allow you to stay at home and die.

By then, I had huge sores all over my tongue and down my throat, and I could hardly swallow. I lay on a bed waiting for the ambulance to arrive and during that time I had to make frequent visits to the bathroom.

The doctor could not believe that on one day I would appear to be completely in control of my life, while the next I appeared to be close to losing my mind.

AND HE SHALL GIVE HIS ANGELS CHARGE OVER THEE

In a short space of time, I began losing my faculties. I remember lying in the surgery waiting for the ambulance to arrive and as I looked up I saw a small angel hovering immediately above my head. As my mind was by then playing all kinds of tricks on me, I was not sure if I could trust my own vision. I rubbed my eyes and looked up. The angel was still there. I rubbed again, and tried to ensure that there was nothing in my eyes to distort the image.

I was amazed. Hovering right over me, was a beautiful little angel. He was about two feet tall and His body appeared to be seated in his wings which were extended. He had a golden white glow and was engulfed in light which was projected all around him. All that I could do was lie there and gazed at it, and this I did until it disappeared.

And He shall give His angels charge over thee to keep thee in all thy ways, they shall bear thee up in their arms lest thou dash thy foot against a stone.
Psalms 91:11 1 2

By the time the ambulance had arrived, I was feeling much better. God had used that angel to watch over me and to strengthen me right there where I lay.

I was taken to London's Guy's hospital, which is one of the top teaching hospitals in London. I had to lie there for the greater part of the day while student doctors came in and out to observe an illness that they may never have seen before in medical history.

My tongue was so swollen and sore that I could neither eat nor swallow, and there were huge bubbles all over it. When I asked the doctor what they were, he was unable to give a proper diagnosis. I believe that they were there as a result of the muck and dirt that those evil spirits had been feeding me with at nights.

Eventually I told the doctor that I was feeling better and that I wished to go home. I had not been treated, because they knew not what to treat me with. When I went home, I had a wonderful dish of hot soup. I had not eaten properly for over six weeks prior to this, and yet here I was enjoying thick hot wonderful soup.

The trial continued however, as for the next few weeks, I regained some strength but continued to be very ill. During that time I was in and out of the doctor's surgery. I found myself on an ECG machine in the hospital as my heart continued to race and I continued to experience a nasty feeling of death in my stomach.

At the same time I was somehow being driven towards food and all that I wanted to do was to eat. I felt that if I didn't eat that I was going to die. In addition I experienced long periods of breathlessness and tiredness because whenever I slept, I was promptly awakened to feel this heavy oppression. Sometimes it would be on top of me and at other times it would be lingering around the home.

I felt as if I was transporting about twenty other people within my body, and eventually began to develop a variety of personalities. I would just burst out crying one minute for no apparent reason. The next minute I felt like there was a smile on my face, and I knew deep down that that smile was not coming from me. I certainly had nothing to be happy about.

Once in my sleep, I was fed with the most awful food that I could have imagined. The next morning I woke up with a dreadful heavy and formidable feeling in my stomach, which cannot be explained.

Despite my numerous trips to the doctor, there was no prescription to ease this problem. The X-rays showed no medical problem and yet I was so ill that I felt as though I was dying.

I did all the possible blood tests to eliminate possible illnesses, including HIV, and I felt a genuine sense of relief when the Doctor called me back to her office. I was confident that by now she would have finally found something that could be treated.

DOCTORS HAVE NO TREATMENT FOR UNCLEAN SPIRITS

It is very difficult to explain to the person who is not ill, how it feels to be afflicted with a sickness that does not have a name and which cannot be treated because there is no treatment for it. I was desperate for the doctor to find something to treat so that I could get back to normal life once again.

With a smile on her face, the Doctor exclaimed:

Lona, I am happy to tell you that nothing is wrong with you! All of your blood tests came back and they are normal!

My heart sank, and looking at her in disappointment I explained that there had to be something there that could be treated.

She concluded that we would have to examine my mental state. I then asked her if she believed in evil spirits and if she thought that that could be what was wrong with me. She did not know what to say, and probably thought that I had lost my mind.

However, by this time, and after all of these futile tests, I was convinced that unclean spirits were living inside of my body. I also knew that these spirits were both vicious and nasty, and that they were assigned to kill me.

It is both tragic and amusing that doctors sit and scratch their heads when they are exposed to evil spirits. The fact is, because they are not aware of the problem, they have no idea what to treat.

Doctors have no treatment for unclean spirits. That s one sickness that they can t deal with. The only way to deal with demonic spirits is through the blood of Jesus, and in the name of Jesus.

Only a blood washed child of God who is filled with the Holy Ghost can effectively cast out demons. Furthermore, those who attempt to do so must be walking in holiness; if they are not, they may find that they leave the demonised person taking some of their spirits with them.

The doctors tried their best but they had not what it takes for them to deal with the demonised. Eventually I ceased going to see them and began to see occultists. By then, I was like a time bomb, which was just waiting to explode.

While all of these things were happening to me, I still had a very demanding job as deputy head of English in one of London's comprehensive schools, and I was still required to carry out those responsibilities. I had taken so much leave from work that I knew then that I was on the verge of losing my job, but this meant nothing to me as I realised that my life was more important than my work.

On the days that I did go to work I would often hear those nasty evil spirits speaking inside of me and telling me to go and kill myself. They told me that I had nothing then to live for and that I would never be well again, and in my desperation I began to travel abroad to see the best occultists, still hoping that they would be able to help me.

For the wages of sin is death but the gift of God is eternal life through Jesus Christ our Lord. ROMANS 6:23

The Bible tells us that: the wages of sin is death and the enemy drew me closer to the threat of certain death with every day that passed. I did not know nor understood, that the Lord was watching over me just as he watches over each one of us.

I did not realise that He was standing by waiting to cleanse me of my sins and to offer me the promise of eternal life in Him. Only Jesus could deliver me from the evil that I was experiencing, and as such these spirits continued to torment me until one glorious day I discovered that my only hope, my healing and my deliverance lay, completely and entirely, in the Lord.

Chapter 5

He came that we might live

'And Jesus arose and followed him, and so did His disciples. And behold a woman, which was diseased with an issue of blood for twelve years, came behind Him and touched the hem of His garment. For she said within herself. If I may but touch His garment, I shall be whole. But Jesus turned Him about and when He saw her he said. 'Daughter, be of good comfort, thy faith hath made thee whole'. And the woman was made whole from that time.' St Matthew 9:19-22

SLEEPING WITH THE ENEMY

As my condition deteriorated, so the evil spirits continued to have their way with me. I was being fed at nights with the worst type of scum imaginable, and I would have vivid dreams of being involved in sexual activities.

The Bible tells us plainly that giants were on the land because of angels having sex with women.

There were giants in the earth in those days: And also After that, when the sons of God came in unto the daughters of men, and they bare children to them. GENESIS 6:4

Angels like these would have been amongst those who were cast out of heaven to join with the host of hell.

They would also belong to the carefully structured legion of darkness that Paul presents to us in the book of Ephesians.

These types of evils are known as incubus and soccubus sexual pervert demons.

If someone were to try to convince me that these sorts of evils existed they would have a difficult task in doing so. However, I have proven these things to be true for myself. The devil had let these evils loose in my own bed and I had no idea of what was happening to me.

As time went by I began to develop this horrible abdominal pains and cervical problems. It was so awful that I had to see the doctor. Once again, they did all the routine checks, only to happily advise me that all was well, that I did had no infections.

I was in continual turmoil and my nervous system was gradually breaking down, as I found that I was unable to think beyond one minute at a time. I had gone to every source I could think of to seek for help, but there was no one who was able to help me.

The nightmares grew worse and worse, and were so dreadful and unbearable, that on reflection I do not know how I had coped with everything that I was going through. I now know that it was the Lord, and His grace that had kept me alive during those nights. Whereas at the time those illnesses were misdiagnosed as panic attacks, I now know them to be The devil s attacks.

I cannot explain to you how ghastly that feeling was. My heart would begin pounding in my chest, and then I would feel the need to quickly grab on to something or someone. I truly felt as though my heart was coming out of my body.

It was a feeling of complete hopelessness, and in short, I felt as though I was about to die. The doctors continued to pump me with tablets that did not work. They even told me to breathe into a bag whenever that happened. Nothing they could give me provided me with a complete cure for that attack of the enemy.

I know that there are many people reading this book who might be suffering from so-called panic attacks and are under the impression that it is only a phobia. I am here to tell you that there is no such sickness as panic attack. This is in truth, an attack of the enemy, and only the Lord can deliver you from such an attack.

THE FAITH TO BELIEVE

My experiences were now becoming similar to those of the woman with the issue of blood. Now note that this woman was bleeding for twelve years. I believe that only the Lord could have saved her life during those years and from her experience we have such an amazing testimony. It must have been traumatic for this woman to struggle with this illness for so long.

The Greek word for issue is '**Rhusis**' which means a flowing . This means that her blood was flowing from her body for years, and as such she must have been physically weak and pale. What she had then would have been described as a bloody flux.

In the book of Leviticus, Moses gave the people his law concerning a woman with such an issue of blood.

And if a woman have an issue of her blood many days out of the time of her separation; All the days of the issue of her uncleanness shall be as the days of her separation: She shall be unclean. Every bed whereon she lieth all the days of her issue shall be unto her as the bed of her separation: Whatsoever she sits upon shall be unclean, as the uncleanness of her separation. And whosoever toucheth those things shall be unclean, and shall wash his clothes, and bathe himself in water and be unclean until the even. But if she be cleansed of her issue, then she shall number to herself seven days and after that she shall be clean. LEVITICUS 16: 25 —28

Not only was this woman very ill, but as a result of her illness she had also become a social outcast. Society would have been looking down upon her because of this illness. I can just picture this woman hiding away from society and being so unhappy with herself.

Something must have really stirred in her when she heard about a man named Jesus who was going about and doing great things.

By this time, Jesus would have stopped in his travels to rebuke the fever from Simons mother, He would have rebuked the unclean spirit out of the Nazarene and the woman would probably have heard about both of these incidents. She would have heard that demons were obeying Jesus and that He was delivering the possessed.

She would have heard of the healing of the leper and of the multitudes that were following Him and that they were being healed. Perhaps she even knew of the Gadarene man whom the Bible says had his dwelling place in the graveyard. Most people would have given up hope of ever seeing that man sane again, so when this woman heard that this demon possessed man was healed, she must have been convinced that Jesus could also do it for her.

She must have been certain that he could heal her issue of blood. There must have been no doubt in her mind. She must have told herself that she would just wait until this man Jesus was passing and that she would just touch His garment. She had built up her faith to such a high level by then that as soon as she touched the hem of His garment faith was released.

As my situation continued I suffered for nearly a year, spent all that I had and was on the verge of giving up. Then one day, in desperation I picked up my Bible and began to read it. I was no expert at praying, but I managed to pray a simple, humble prayer to the Lord daily.

THE POWER OF PRAYER AND FASTING

Each morning I would pick up the Bible and would read the first text that came to me. One morning I opened the Bible to read and the chapter that I opened it to was Matthew 17. I read it until I came to verse fourteen, and I read it through to verse 21 which read:

And when they were come to the multitude, there came to Him a certain man kneeling and saying, Lord have mercy on my son for He is lunatic and sore vexed, for oftentimes he falleth into the fire and oft into the water. And I bought him to thy disciples and they could not cure him.

Then Jesus answered and said Oh faithless and perverse generation, how long shall I suffer you? Bring him hither to me. And Jesus rebuked the devil and it departed out of him. And the child was cured from that very hour.

Then came the disciples to Jesus apart and said why could not we cast him out? And Jesus said unto them because of your unbelief:

For verily I say unto you, if ye have faith as a grain of mustard, ye shall say unto this mountain, Remove hence to yonder place and it shall be move, and nothing shall be impossible unto you . Howbeit this kind goeth not out but prayer and fasting. St Matthew 17: 14-21

I read that scripture, and for the first time, the Bible became alive to me. I felt like I heard the voice of God speaking to me through those pages. I could clearly hear the Lord saying to me:

You are possessed with evil spirits, and they are some vicious and nasty ones. They will only leave through prayer and fasting.

I did not know how to fast and even if I did, I was too ill to do so. Moreover, if I did not eat every hour I felt that I could not live. I had blown up like a balloon and my hair had begun to fall out. I looked terrible.

I continued to read the Bible for comfort and as I did my faith continued to grow. I was still deteriorating but I was holding on to the Bible. In truth, I was seeking for comfort and consolation in the words of God, and yet I was not seeking for God.

Eventually I heard the Lord speaking to me once again. He told me that I needed Him and not just the Bible. I began to pray asking the Lord to come into my heart. As I began to find peace in the Lord I felt as Paul must have felt in that Roman prison when he said:

For to me to live is Christ and to die is gain . PHILIPPIANS. 1:21.

I decided that if the Lord were to spare my life, then I would not want to do anything that would be outside of His will. Also, that if I should die then I wouldn't want to spend the rest of my life with someone as cruel as the devil. I made the conscious decision to repent, and I asked the Lord to come into my heart.

One morning I opened the Bible to read it and I landed on James chapter five. When I got to verse 16 the words seemed to jump out of the page. It read:

The effectual fervent prayer of a righteous man availeth much.
JAMES 5:16

I immediately saw the relationship between this verse and Matthew 17:21-24, where Jesus speaks of the need for prayer and fasting. I realised that in order to make a full recovery I needed a righteous man, or men and women of God to pray for me who were also fasting.

As such I changed the way in which I was praying, and where I had formerly been praying for healing, I now prayed that the Lord would send me a righteous person who could pray for me. Everyday, I would pray:

Lord, please send me a righteous person.

A COVENANT WITH THE FATHER

There were days when those evil spirits would torment me so much that I felt like walking and walking. In fact there were times when they would tell me to go for a long walk and I would obey. At that time I was seeking for God and to me a church was just a church, I never knew nor understood the differences between denominations, as far as I was concerned, God lived in churches.

There was a Catholic Church just down the road from me, and whenever those spooks sent me walking, I would end up in that Church hall and I would sit there and pray.

One morning I went there to find solace and somehow amidst the idols hanging around me, the smell of incense and the stench of candles burning, right in the midst of that idol worship, I found the Lord. I went to the altar and knelt to pray and the tears began to flow as I emptied my heart out to the Lord and begged for forgiveness.

I had found myself in a desperate situation. I had five beautiful children who loved and needed their mother so much, and yet I was staring death in the face. I knew I had to live for them and so, in my desperation, I cried out to the Lord and made my everlasting covenant with Him.

I told the Lord that if He were to spare my life, then I would serve Him until I die.

Chapter 6

For Better or Worse,
Not Even in Death do us Part

Wherefore they are no more two, but one flesh What God has joint together let no man put asunder
Matthew 19:6

YOU ARE FEARFULLY AND WONDERFULLY MADE

As I knelt at that alter in the chapel, I was so broken. I heard the quiet feet of nuns passing behind me as I sobbed my heart out to the Lord. I imagine that as they stopped and looked at me they would have said a little prayer, such as Lord have mercy on that poor soul , made the sign of the cross and moved on.

However, little did they know, that I was no longer a poor soul. I had just found the richest person in the whole wide world. I was having my engagement party and was about to tie the knot - for better or worse, in sickness and in health, not even in death do us part!

I did not see the candles burning neither did I smell the stench of burning wax. I had no fear, but instead I had complete peace because I had just found Jesus. I do not know how long I spent on my knees but when I got up, I felt a peace that I could not explain. The glory of God was all over me.

I got up and quietly walked past those statues and went home. I had just unknowingly, with no experience of teachings on covenanting and only vague scriptural understanding, covenanted with the Lord. I have learned since then that God is everywhere and that all that we need to do is to reach out and touch Him.

Although my physical condition was gradually improving, I was still quite unwell. Those stubborn demons were not prepared to leave without a fight. I had found the Lord but I needed someone to guide me.

About six weeks after making my covenant with the Lord, I started to recover and I decided to go back to work. I had a very demanding job, and I did not feel confident enough to discuss my illness with anyone at work, especially as I did not

31

want to be considered weird . Besides, I was too ill to hold any substantial conversation and as such I tried my best to avoid interaction. I felt like a social outcast, but I had an assurance that the Lord was with me and that gave me comfort.

There were times when I would be teaching a lesson and I would hear the evil voices telling me to go and kill myself and finish with my life. They would jeer at me saying, Don t you see that your life is finished? while they asked me what the reason was that I wanted to live for. I can remember one day as I was standing in front of my class, I heard those evils telling me that I should go and throw myself on a nearby train line, so that I could be relieved of all the pain, worry and fear.

Thankfully, instead of running to the train line, I ran to a lady s house for prayer.

On another occasion I was on the bus going to work when evil spirits came on the bus with me and told me that I should throw myself off the bus while it was moving. I just sat there as calmly as I could and found the strength to hang on to myself with all that was within me.

With this continual attack I was fast becoming a nervous wreck and my mind kept going around and around like the second hand of a clock. I had to learn to keep control by limiting my thinking to one minute at a time and by focusing myself by silently repeating: The blood of Jesus! The blood of Jesus! The blood of Jesus! The name of Jesus! In the name of Jesus! In the name of Jesus! I found that an air of calm would quietly come over me as soon I began repeating those words.

There were some days when I would lock myself away in my classroom in the daytime and pray to the Lord. I continued to ask Him to send me a righteous man, but when He answered my prayer, instead He sent both righteous men and women.

HE SENT ME RIGHTEOUS PEOPLE

For many are called but few are chosen. St Matthew 21:16 & St Matthew 22:14

I know that there are people reading this book who are going through depression. They may feel that they have come to the end of their tether and as though, they should give up. Others may suffer from addictions, and may be hooked on drugs, alcohol, sex, fraud or other binding affliction. They may be feeling that life has nothing to offer them and may be considering putting an end to their suffering by committing suicide. Those who are experiencing these trials should consider instead what David says in the book of Psalms:

I am fearfully and wonderfully made. PSALMS 139:14

You are fearfully and wonderfully created. Before the foundation of the earth, the Lord knew you. He saw you when you were nothing but sperm. You were fighting amongst millions of others for survival. In addition, you could have been among the ones that have died. However, God had a purpose for your life and so he called you into being.

He did not just call you to be a drug addict; neither did He call you to be a prostitute. The bible says that your body is the temple of the living God. He did not make you to be depressed, sad or lonely. Those problems are all the schemes of the enemy. You are in satan s territory and that is why you are suffering. He has captured you. But I am here to tell you that Jesus came to set the captive free and that you do not have to suffer anymore.

I want you to be aware that the Lord will not judge you according to your past. If He were to do that, then we would not have had an Apostle Paul to lay the foundation for the wonderful New Testament Church. Neither would we have the marvellous revelation of the Kingdom of God that he has given so beautifully to us in his writings.

Paul was formerly the great persecutor of the churches and had caused the imprisonment and death of many of the early days believers. However, when the Lord called him on the road to Damascus, he was not only given eyes that could see things spiritually but God also gave him a change of name. God immediately took all his sins and dumped them into the sea of forgetfulness.

Everyone might know your identity now and they will surely categorise you with what you are doing. Nevertheless, I just want you to know that when the Lord calls you he will give you a new identification card and His name will be written on it along with yours. Above that will be written:

Elect for the Kingdom of God!

Thank God it does not matter what you were then, or what you were doing then, for although your sins are as crimson, He will make you clean.

Rehab was described as a harlot in the book of Joshua chapter one. Although she was the owner of a brothel, it was she who helped the Israelites to conquer the Canaanites in the battle of Jericho. Furthermore, if you examine the book of Matthew, chapter one, you will find her mentioned in the genealogy of Jesus Christ.

David was such a sinful man that sin seemed an addiction in his life, but each time that he sinned he would return to the Lord with a contrite heart and ask for forgiveness. In Psalm 51 he says to the Lord:

Have mercy upon me oh Lord according to thy loving kindness according unto the multitude of thy tender mercies blot out my transgressions. Wash me from mine iniquities and cleanse me from my sins. Psalm 51:1

In verse 10, he says:

Create in me a clean heart oh God and renew a right spirit within me. Cast me not away from thy presence and take not thy Holy Spirit from me. Restore unto me the joy of thy salvation and uphold me with thy free spirit . Psalms 51:1 & 10-1

David knows that our God is a just God.

Paul tells us in Galatians 1:15, that the Lord had separated him, that is, set him aside for the work of the Lord, since he was in his mother s womb.

You too have been separated since you were in your mother s womb and just like David you are fearfully and wonderfully created and God has a purpose for your life. When you cast your burdens unto the Lord, He takes them and dumps them into the sea of forgetfulness never to be retrieved.

No matter what you are going through in this life, Jesus is your only answer. I was in a similar position to what you may be going through. I was so broken up and confused that I did not know what to do. I had tried everything and nothing could help. I had been abroad looking for help from the best occultists. I tried the best spells on the market that I could get hold of.

I visited medical professors, and was placed on ECG machines. At times I could actually feel my heart racing against my ribs and there were moments when I felt that it was about to stop beating. I was told that I was suffering from panic attack, was given tablets, and was told to breathe in a bag whenever I had an attack. These methods did not help. In fact whenever the feeling took me I just wanted to run away. I just wanted to find an escape route.

I remember looking at elderly people in the streets and feeling that they were in a far better situation than I was in. As far as I was concerned, they were only suffering from old age. It was the same if I saw someone with a broken leg or arm, as I was convinced that every other situation was better than my own. Those bones could be repaired, but I felt that what I was experiencing was beyond repair. I saw myself in a desperate situation of no return.

THE JOY OF DELIVERANCE

One day I went to a teacher-training course. During those times, I would try to avoid holding long conversations, as I could not speak for more than about two minutes at a time. I was sitting alone having lunch, when a colleague came over to me and asked if she could share my lunch. I had just finished eating so we had a laugh about that. She said that she would like to come and visit me at home that evening and I agreed.

I was in bed when she came. During those times I was so ill that I would rush home from work and go straight to my bed. I invited her up to my bedroom and we sat talking for a short while. Then she boldly said to me, Lona, I ve come to tell you that you are under spiritual attack.

To say that I was surprised is a mild way of putting it. I was flabbergasted. I never knew that she understood anything about spiritual attack.

I realised immediately that the Lord had sent someone that I could talk to and I began to pour out my heart to her. Through flowing tears I told her what had happened to me. She listened carefully, and then told me that her sister was a member of an apostolic church and that she would speak with her to arrange for a group of Born Again Christians to come and offer me deliverance. The appointment was set and I waited anxiously for a whole week until I could see these people.

Once again, I am reminded of the woman with the issue of blood. Having been through this experience I can imagine this woman eagerly waiting for the Lord to pass her way. The more that she heard of miracles, the more her faith grew.

As the doctors had failed this woman, she may well have gone to the occultists just as I had, and they too would have failed her. In her desperation of having no one else to turn to she would have heard that Jesus was coming her way. Jesus would have been her last hope. She had no money left and no options left to try after twelve years of searching. If Jesus could not help her, then she would surely die.

I was also in a position where all had failed me and Jesus had became my only hope. My final hope came through hearing that people were passing my way that had the authority to deliver me from the realm of darkness.

As I sat waiting my faith was growing. I knew in my spirit that if the Lord couldn t help me then, I was going to die. Eventually the day came. There was a group of about six people who came from the Bible way apostolic Church in Lewisham. They held a short counselling session with me before they began. They realised that I had already accepted the Lord as my saviour and that I was willing to sever all ungodly links with the realm of darkness and so they set to work.

This has to be one of the most glorious days of my life. One group was praying in tongues while the next was praying in their earthly languages. I just love the song, which says that Burdens are lifted at Calvary.

I was at Calvary that day, and I was being soaked in the blood of Jesus. It went over my body, it penetrated my pores, went through the capillaries into the veins through the blood stream and right into my heart. It pumped through my body, searching for the demons that had to run when Jesus came.

I felt the blood of Jesus searching for them and I felt them running. Thank God, Jesus will not share house with the devil. He walked in as the rightful occupant and all aliens had to go.

It was sheer glory, and mere words just cannot explain how it felt. I was washed and washed and washed and then I found myself speaking a beautiful language. I m speaking it as I am writing this book, but unfortunately I can t write that one down as men cannot read it and they can t understand it for that one goes beyond human comprehension. It goes straight to the throne room of God in heaven. Oh hallelujah! Glory be to God!

When demons hear that language, they have to flee and principalities have to move. The devil himself has to take his leave because He cannot stand in the presence of the Holy Spirit.

The spirit that came to dwell in me that day is not a familiar spirit. It is the one and only inimitable Holy Spirit. Occultists don t have it, spiritualists don t have it, mediums don t have it, clairvoyants can t have it, tea gazers can t have it, card readers don t know it, witches don t have it and devils don t have it. It is special, it is pure, and it is wonderful because it is a Holy Spirit. It does not apply to the lord of the flies or to that of the dunghill. It flows from the throne room of God.

I basked in the presence of the Lord as the angels ministered to me. It was just beautiful. During that illness, my stomach became enlarged. That day, it went right down. Even my countenance changed.

I was now a new creature in Christ. Old things had passed away, and now all things have become new.

When I was able to speak, I asked the men and women of God if they had been fasting. 'Yes! they answered. They were praying people and not only were they in prayer and fasting, but they had come to deliver me under divine instruction. God had sent them to set this captive free. Glory be to God I am free at last.
The Bible says:

Repent and be baptised every one of you in the name of the Lord Jesus Christ for the remission of your sins and ye shall receive the gift of the Holy Ghost. ACTS 2:38.

Once you have accepted the Lord then you just want to be baptised and be filled with the Holy Spirit. If I had been able to I would have been baptised right there and then, but instead I had to wait for a long week because there was no pool in my house.

I now have Jesus and that is one person that no one can take away from me. I thank Jesus continually for loving me so much that He would sacrifice Himself so that I could be free. Without him I would still be living my life in torment and those demons would still be attacking me in the quiet of my mind, in my thoughts and in my dreams and no one else could help me.

Jesus said that He came that we may live , and now I have dedicated my life to Him completely, for better for worse until death and beyond. Thank God for the deliverance that comes through, and only through Christ Jesus our Lord.

Chapter 7

Free At Last

'He that dwelleth in the secret place of the most high shall abide under the shadows of the almighty
Psalm 91

DWELLING IN THE SECRET PLACE

The days and months ahead were amongst the most trying times for me. If you are reading this book and you are a babe in Christ, or a new convert, I would like to encourage you to hang in there. I realise that this may be the most trying experience for you.

The enemy will try to remind you of every foolish thing in the world that you are walking away from. As you continue to grow with the Lord, those things will fade and lose their value, and in Jesus you will have something far more valuable that you will treasure so much more and that will last forever.

Each time that the enemy sees you living in God s victory with the promise of eternal life and complete peace and happiness with the Father, he is reminded of what he had before he traded it in for pride and greed.

His sole aim now is to see if he can get you back into his slave market. Satan had you redeemed by corruptible things, but you are now redeemed not by gold and silver but by the precious blood of Jesus.

I would like to remind you of that lively hope that the apostle Peter tells us about. He says that you are:

begotten into a lively hope, by the resurrection of Jesus Christ from the dead to an inheritance, incorruptible and undefiled and that fadeth not away reserved in heaven for y o u * 1 Peter 1:4

What an assurance! Paul says that if it were only in this life that we had a hope then we would be men most miserable. It is so important for you to remember as a young Christian that you are selected, and that you are special, so hang in there.

Peter further tells us that we as children of God are:

A chosen generation, a royal priesthood, a holy nation, a peculiar people. That we should show forth the praises to Him who hath called you out of darkness into His marvellous light. 1 Peter 2:9

I know that you must have had some hard times out there in the world, but stay mindful of what the Lord has delivered you from. Give thanks to God at all times, knowing that had it not been for his mercies, satan would have had you under his feet like grapes.

Remember that you are not alone. When I was newly saved, the Lord led me to Psalm 91.

He that dwelleth in the secret place of the most high shall abide under the shadows of the almighty. I will say of the Lord He is my refuge and my fortress my God in Him will I trust. Surely He shall deliver thee from the snare of the fowler and from the noisome pestilence. He shall cover thee with His feathers and under His wings shall thou trust His truth shall be thy shield and buckler. Thou shalt not be afraid for the terror that flieth by night nor for the arrow that flieth by day, nor for the pestilence that walketh in darkness, nor the destruction that wasteth at noonday. A thousand shall fall at thy side and ten thousand at they right hand but it shall not come nigh thee. Only with thine eyes shalt thou behold and see the reward of the wicked because thou hast made the Lord even the most high God thy habitation. There shall no evil befall thee neither shall any plagues come nigh thy dwelling. For He shall give His angels charge over thee to keep thee in all thy ways. They shall bear thee up in their hands lest thou dash thy foot against a stone. Thou shalt tread upon the lion and adder the young lion and the dragon shalt thou trample under feet Because he hath set his love upon thee therefore will I deliver him. I will set him on high , because he hath known my name. He shall call upon me and I shall answer him. I will be with him in trouble, I will deliver him, and honour him. With long life will I satisfy him and show him my salvation. Psalm 91

These words gave me both strength and comfort as I held onto God through the devil s attacks. It was my solace when principalities and powers were assigned to kill me. It was my comfort when I couldn t sleep at nights.

At times when I felt that all the hosts of hell had built strongholds around my home and my life, it was my sustenance. It was my comfort as a new Christian and it is still my consolation today.

Lets look at the first two verses.

He that dwelleth in the secret place of the most high shall abide under the shadow of the Almighty. PSALMS 91:1 & 2

The Hebrew word for dwell is yashab, and it means to sit down, to dwell, to remain or to settle in the sense of taking out a homestead or staking out a claim and resisting all claim jumpers. It also means, to possess a place and to live there.

The Hebrew word for Almighty there is Shadday. When it appears as El shadday it means God almighty. The Patriarchs of the Old Testament used it to mean mighty unconquerable. It is also used, as a compound of the particle sheh meaning which or who and day meaning sufficient. Shedday or Shadday is therefore the all-sufficient God.

These verses are saying that when you are living in the word of the Lord, and you put your trust in Him, believe in Him, live in His presence and make Him your only God, then He will protect you because He is the all-sufficient God. He is mighty and He is unconquerable.

When you dwell somewhere then you permanently stay there. Unfortunately some folks are visitors to the secret place of the most high. And they only make their infrequent visits when they are in trouble and therefore the enemy is aware of this.

He will therefore heap problems upon problems upon your head because he is well aware of the fact that you do not live there, that you are only a guest. The psalmist is saying that we should not be visitors to the secret place, but that instead we should be resident occupants. We should live in the throne room of God Almighty.

Shortly after my deliverance, the enemies returned, and this time they came back with forces that were more evil than them. There was no questioning the fact that I was now a blood washed Christian, but I was also a babe in Christ who knew nothing about putting on the whole armour of God.

PROTECTING YOURSELF AND GUARDING AGAINST THE ENEMY

Through the power of the Lord that was invested in them, this wonderful group of saved people was able to deliver me from the kingdom of darkness. I became a member of the church, was attending regular services and was dwelling in the presence of the Lord. However, I needed more, I needed to understand what I was fighting with and how I could protect myself daily against such forces.

You see it is wonderful to be saved. But when you are coming out of the kingdom of darkness and especially if you know secrets about the devils works, you pose a threat to his kingdom because you can expose secrets that can be detrimental to his dark regime. In these cases you need much more than baby food. You need to be watched over daily. I was now on my own, but thanks be to God, angels were assigned to take care of me.

When the enemies came against me at nights, I found solace in the fact that I was now serving a mighty conquering God who was protecting me. Armed with that knowledge, I was able to conquer fear. As long as you are hiding under the shadows of the wings of the Almighty, be assured that the Lord is protecting you.

Verse three says that:

He shall deliver you from the snare of the fowler and from the noisome pestilence. He shall cover thee with his feathers and under his wings shalt thou trust. His truth shall be thy shield and buckler.

One night after my deliverance, I woke to see the figure of a man standing over my bed with his back towards me. His form was so big and wide that it almost took up the whole width of the room. He was dressed like a shepherd wearing a headdress, similar to that worn in the Middle East, and he held a shepherd s rod in his hand. As I lay there looking at this person, he gradually began to disappear.

I felt no fear, but rather, complete peace and tranquillity as I quietly went back to sleep. The Lord was covering me under His wings. In the book of John 10:11 He says:

I am the good shepherd and the good shepherd taketh care of his sheep

What an awesome assurance. The Lord had revealed Himself to me as my Jehovah Rohi, the Lord my Shepherd.

If we could always keep one beautiful thought in our mind, that the Lord loves us to the extent that He has given His life for us, then we would know that there is no need to worry.

Can you imagine loving someone so much that you are prepared to give up your life, to die for that person? That is what I call real agape, self-sacrificing love. Greater love hath no man than that.

David tells us further in the psalm that:

we should not be afraid for the terror by night. Nor for the arrow that flieth by day, nor for the pestilence that walketh in darkness. Nor for the destruction that wasteth at noonday. He says that a thousand shall fall at thy side and ten thousand at thy right hand but it shall not come nigh thee.

It is clear from these verses that in the days of David, people often suffered from demonic attack. Demonology was also a taught subject in Hebrew theology at the time of Christ s advent. (See Matt. 9:34 and in the Great Commission: Mark 16: 15-18).

This passage promises protection from sickness, as one of the blessings, which are afforded to those who are redeemed. The Hebrew word for plague is nehgahand and is used to refer to something inflicted on the body and specifically used to refer to spots and leprosy. The Lord is here offering us protection against diseases, but this is conditional on us first making the Lord our refuge and habitation.

The means by which we do so, is found in two Hebrew words in verse 9. The word Makhesh translated refuge means a shelter and also a place of trust. It is derived from the root word khawsaw, meaning to flee for protection or to confide in. Maween, translated dwelling, speaks of a retreat and comes from the root onah and describes an intimate relationship, dwelling together as in marriage.

This therefore is telling us that when we make the Lord our habitation by trusting in Him, taking all of our worries to Him; our fears and our heartaches, our pains and our needs. By seeking counsel from the Lord, spending quality time in prayer and fasting with Him, thanking Him, loving Him and walking close to Him daily. Then He will take us into a sheltered place of promise regarding our health, our prosperity, against the evil ones, against all our problems and we will receive His mercy.

After my deliverance, I prayed to the Lord daily, I presented my case to Him in prayer and supplication and I gave thanks for all things.

I began to walk with the Lord and He became my refuge and my shelter. I realised that I had to also cover my children and so I did. I found out that all the little money that I had, had disappeared, so I had to ask the Lord for a new income and not only that, I had to safeguard it with prayer.

I realised that the Lord was calling me to leave my job and to focus on Him. I realised that some things have to go when you receive the Lord, and that when He wants to bring you into a safe place of peace and security, He will take away from you the things that might hinder you from fulfilling your purpose. John 3:30 says:

He must increase, but I must decrease. John 3 :30

The job went but I was left with something that money could not buy. I still have that and I m holding on to it more securely than before. In verses 11 and 12, David tells us that:

The Lord shall give His angels charge over thee to keep thee in all thy ways, that They shall bear thee up in their hands. Lest thou dash thy foot against a stone.

My healing was not completed in one day. It took one day for the demons to leave my body. While they had been inside me they had destroyed my health in the process, and it took a while for me to be nurtured back to health. Many nights they would try to return to damage me, but I was no longer in satan s slave market, and I could stand boldly in the word of God.

One night as I was sleeping, I witnessed a creature which resembled a cobra trying to make it s way into my bed and I shouted to it, You can t touch me now, I m a child of a King, I m a princess! It was as though my voice had echoed out in the ethos.

It seemed as though the devil didn t realise that by then I had come to know about my redeemer. I am reminded of Job in the book of Job chapter 19. After all of the unbearable trials he endured, some would have thought that he would have done what his wife told him to do, Curse God and die

But Job said:

For I know that my redeemer liveth, and that He shall stand at the latter day upon the earth. And though after my skin worms destroy this body. Yet in my flesh shall I see God. Whom I shall see for myself and mine eyes shall behold and not another. Though my reins be consumed within me. Job 19:25-27.

For the next few weeks, I had to hold on to the Lord with all that was within me. I realised that Rebecca Brown's Elaine in her book He Came to Set the Captive Free was lucky that she had Rebecca to help her. Elaine had been under serious spiritual attack and God used Rebecca to rescue her from the evil forces of darkness.

I had no one but the Lord to help me and because of that I had to go through in the toughest way. You see I couldn't see then, but the Lord was making a deliverance minister of me and I had to do it on my own, and only with His guidance.

There were times when demons came and fed me in my sleep although I was delivered and I had to learn how to stop eating dirty spiritual food. They still made their way into my bed and I had to learn for myself how to stop that. I was delivered but was left with many strongholds and open doorways in my life which were entrances for demons to continue creeping in and out and I had to take the authority for myself, kick those demons out and close those doors.

I had to learn how to do it for myself, so that I could do it for others. As we look at the deliverance process in later chapters we will review in detail what we must do to ensure that we are completely free from all attacks of the enemy.

During this period I was in training in one of God's greatest universities and I just did not realise. In retrospect I can now say that my sufferings were not in vain. You see the Lord has a way of using the little dirty schemes of the devil and turning them around for His good and purpose. Now I cannot say that I am sorry that I went through all of those things, because my experience is leading so many wounded souls to Christ.

VISIONS OF DESTINY

One night, I had such a dreadful attack from the enemy that I thought that I was not going to live. The oppression around the house was so strong that it was actually stifling. I prayed and prayed and struggled to sleep. That night I had one of the most beautiful experiences of my life.

In my deep sleep, I heard angels singing to me. This is the most melodious of voices that I had ever heard in my life. The words to the song that they were singing were as follows:

> I'm on the battlefield for my Lord
> I'm on the battlefield for my Lord

I promise that I would

Serve him till I die

So I m on the battle field for my Lord.

They sang and sang and sang. And as I was coming back to reality, they were disappearing. I just didn t want them to go. I listened until the voices disappeared into the distance. I tried to go back to sleep hoping that I would hear them again but I wasn t that fortunate.

Another night I went to heaven. This was a very vivid experience. I must have been dosing off to sleep, when I felt myself slip out of my body and began to move upward at a very fast rate. I went through two heavens before reaching the third one. The first heaven was quite cold and dismal and I saw no life form there, so I quickly moved on.

The second heaven was quite chaotic, there were some weird beings there and it was so horrible and frightening that I quickly moved on to the third heaven. When I got there, I saw a huge gate. This gate was made of gold at the top and another material of dark glassy colour at the bottom. It was very wide and it arched in the middle.

There was an angel standing at the gate on guard at one of the far ends. He didn t look at me but stood quietly. At the other end was another angel in the same position.

Above the gate was a huge sign, which read:

 Celestial city, you may enter .

The gates swung open and I stepped in. I knew that I was in heaven. I was expecting to see streets of gold as I had heard, but there were no streets of gold. Just ordinary beautiful streets, and real grass, which I had walked on. For some unknown reason, I did not go beyond the first court.

As I stood there I saw a little girl walked up to me and greeted me. She asked me if I recognised her and I told her that I did not. She told me that she was my sister who had died before I was born. She told me her name and I told her that I had heard my mother speak of her. She proceeded to tell me that I had great callings upon my life and was giving me instructions as to how to behave in this life.

While she was speaking to me, I became aware that something was playing with my hand on earth. She pointed that out to me and told me that I should return immediately to protect my body. Because my spirit had left my body, unclean spirits must have seen this as an opportunity to come in. The division between the spirit and the body is discussed in more detail in the chapter on Strongholds.

What amazed me was the beauty, holiness and tranquillity of the place.

I am not saying that there are no streets of gold in heaven. Heaven is a very big place and I only went to the forefront received the message that I went for and returned, but I saw and felt a peace there that I have never experienced in my whole life. The beauty was unspeakable.

Another night I had a vision of being transported to the river Jordan. The gentleman who came for me told me that he was under instructions to take me to the river Jordan. I went there with him in his very antique car. I have not seen such a car in this life. I heard the great roaring of the river before reaching my destination.

When I got there it was a most-frightening experience, the water was descending out of very long, high and wide mountain range, which was about ten miles wide into a very large river across which I could not see the other side from where I was standing.

As the water pitched down, it was foaming and it made such a terrible deafening noise that I was afraid to look. By this time, I was no longer in the car and stood looking at the river in fear. I quickly turned to tell the gentleman that I couldn't cross alone. I'm sorry!, he shouted, You have to cross Jordan alone! And with that he drove off, leaving me there wondering what I should do.

I decided that I was going to walk back because I could not cross those terrible waters, however when I tried to walk back I found that I was standing facing thickets and a great mountain range that I could not climb. The gentleman was nowhere in sight. There was no way that I could walk back. I had two choices. It was either that I would sit there until I die or jump off into the water.

I jumped into the water but I do not remember swimming - in fact I cannot even swim. Yet I found myself shortly after taking that step, sitting at peace on the other side.

In another vision, the Lord took me on a journey to hell. When I got there I saw people lying in trenches of muck. I did not see the fire, but there was torment everywhere. Every one seemed as though they had gone crazy and were just constantly tearing themselves. They lay in dirty smelly trenches and were all in rags. I did not feel the heat, but I am sure that there was a dreadful heat there from the manner in which they where tearing at themselves.

They all seemed so deranged and confused that all I wanted to do was to get out of there as fast as possible and to run for my life. Hell is the most dreadful place imaginable.

Other people who have been there have spoken of the fire that they saw. All that I saw was indescribable torment and a place that no one would want to go to. I am sure that there is constant fire burning in hell, but I also knew that I was on a guided tour and subsequently would have been protected from the heat and also from the fire.

These experiences were all part of the training that I have received from the Lord during my recuperation. The Lord took me through those experiences so that I could return to warn men of the terrible fate, which awaits them in hell if they did not repent, and of the joy that awaits them in glory, when they submit their lives to God.

The truth is that we all have to cross Jordan alone. We love our children, our parents and partners, but they cannot cross with us. We don t cross as couples we cross as individuals. But when we live a clean life on earth here we know that Jesus will be waiting for us on the other side, to take us in His arms to Glory.

Oh if men could understand the dreadfulness of hell and repent of their sins before it s too late! If they could understand that after the evil one is finished with them then it s certain death! If in this life they could have a vision of hell then they would have an understanding of what it means, and why we need to be Christians.

During that period of bitter illness, God could have turned his back on me. After all, I deserved all that I had been through; I had turned my back on the Lord. If as His child for whom He has given His life, you decide to turn your back on Him, then why shouldn t He chastise you? I can now only thank God that He does not judge us according to our past experiences, and that once again I can declare through Him that I am truly, Free at Last.

Chapter 8

Chosen Without a Choice

You have not chosen me but I have chosen you and have ordained you that ye shall go and bring forth fruit and that the fruit should remain that whatseoever ye shall ask of the father in my name, He shall give you.
John 15:16

THE CALL TO MINISTRY

Like Jonah, who had a calling upon his life, we sometimes think that we can run away from the Lord. When He calls us for service, we sometimes tend to look for an easy way out. However, David in his affliction asks the question in Psalms 139.

Whither shall I go from thy spirit? Or whither shall I go from thy presence? If I ascend up into heaven thou art there. If I make my bed in hell, behold thou art there. If I take the wings of the morning, and dwell in the uttermost part of the sea, even there shall thy hand lead me and thy right hand shall hold me.
PSALMS 139:7-9

If the hand of the Lord is upon us, then we just cannot run. No matter where we go, he ll find us. When we try to run from God then we are only trying to create trouble for ourselves and He will create a storm in our lives.

When the Lord called me for service, I began to run. How could I do the work of the Lord when everyone knew me as a psychic? Would they believe that I was really called by the Lord? I was trying to be pleasers of men and not of God.

Each time that I heard the Lord calling me I would not heed to that call for service. Like Jonah, I was running. Nevertheless, one day the voice of the Lord came to me so audible that I could not resist it. He told me that I should set up a ministry.

I frankly told him that I could not for the same reasons that I ve listed above. Then, in an open vision, the Lord gave me the whole composition and augmentation of the church. He said to me:

People will be still coming to you for psychic work, but you must not turn them away, you should tell them about me. You should also begin a prayer group with them.

Then he gave me another open vision of an eagle spreading its wings and flying away seeking food for its young ones.

I saw the little ones in the nest as the mother went out in search of food and returned with it in its beak for them. Then the Lord said to me:

Lona, you will no longer walk but you will fly, I have now given you wings and you will mount up with wings like an eagle.

It was so awesome that I began to cry, and the more that I thought about it was the more that I cried. I was called to ministry and there was nowhere to run. I had to obey the voice of the Lord.

For the following weeks ahead I was walking as though I was in another world. I felt like I was transporting a very heavy burden. One day I walked into a shoe shop and there I met a lady. We began talking and I told her of the burden that was on me. She went away and prayed and the next time that I saw her, she bore witness with me that the Lord had called me to ministry.

By the next time that I saw her I was telling her of a little church in the vineyard that the Lord was adding to its number daily, where souls were being baptised with the Holy Spirit, and of a group of twenty people who were ready for watery baptism.

OUR GOD IS A GOD OF ORDER

I soon realised that that lady was an apostolic woman of God and that her church came under the Pentecostal assembly of the world. Therefore, the first thing that the Lord did was to place us under the umbrella of a church, and as the church emerged, so the miracles began. Demons were being cast out, diseases were being healed and souls were being baptised with the Holy Spirit.

People came from all walks of life for deliverance and they were receiving it, but above all they were receiving the Lord as their personal saviour. Some of the testimonies of those whom God has used us to deliver may be found in the final chapter of this book.

However, I would like to move on from here to deal with the subject of the deliverance ministry and spiritual warfare, as this is the real purpose of this book. The personal testimony I have outlined so far is a living example, and is most significant because it is upon the foundation of those experiences that the Lord has enabled me to form a successful deliverance ministry.

I am quite aware that deliverance and spiritual warfare is a very controversial area of ministry. This controversy is another attempt at deception by the enemy who would like us to forget that he is out there creating havoc in people s lives; destroying the lives of our children; disrupting our work places, and making our jobs more difficult; breaking up our families and infiltrating our finances.

He has allowed many of our children to become social outcasts and delinquents, and has formulated such terms as maladjusted and malfunctional, which are being used to describe our wonderful children. He has been using the media, politicians, movie stars, and other great personalities to infiltrate evil into our homes.

He is pulling down churches, breaking up relationships, have our children on drugs, wreaking havoc on the streets with prostitution and all sorts of sexual immoralities. He is riding on the airwaves and is coming into our homes through the television in the form of pornographic films, horror movies and now in children games. His last and worst onslaught is to possess the minds of people, sending then to mental homes and to an early grave.

Therefore, he wants this great area of the gospel to be hidden or to be ignored so that he can continue to create destruction. Regardless of his intentions, we do not serve a mute God who is happy to sit and watch while satan creates havoc in the lives of His people.

God is coming back at him by raising up an end time army that is militant, vicious, ferocious and angry, and who are not stopping at any old thing.

We have not come to sit pretty in the pew. We are warriors for Christ. We have no time for spiritual empires. We do not want to be movie stars, nor do we have time for pretty talk. We have come to the Lord with blood in a we eyes, and the sword of God in our hands. and we mean business for the King in this end time.

I used to be a fighter out there, but now I now have an adversary and all anger has been switched to him and his foul spirits.

I can hear a Holy war cry in the heavenly. The kingdom of God has been suffering violence for too long and we now have to take back cities for God by force!!!

It is no time to sit feeling sorry for ourselves. God is calling us to the battlefront, and the devil had better watch out, because we are saddling up ourselves to take the cities of this earth for Him.

Chapter 9

Spiritual Warfare:
How it all began

"How art thou fallen from heaven, o Lucifer son of the morning! How art thou cast down to the ground, which did weaken the nations! For thou hast said in thine heart, I will ascend into heaven. I will exalt my throne above the stars of God. I will sit also upon the heights of the clouds. I will be like the most high. Yet thou shalt be brought down to hell to the sides of the pit. They that see thee shall narrowly look upon thee, saying, is this the man that made the earth tremble that did shake kingdoms. That made the world as a wilderness and destroyed the cities thereof, that opened the house of his prisoner?' Isaiah 14 : 12 –17.

THE ANGEL THAT DESIRED TO DETHRONE GOD

The above verses give us an insight into what must have been one of the most ferocious demonstrations of spiritual warfare that was ever fought. Lucifer, before being cast out of heaven, was a most beautiful angel. So handsome was he that he was known as the the son of the morning . To his disdain, he fell into pride and self-centredness, and foolishly sought to overthrow the God who had created him.

In planning his corrupt and ill-conceived rebellion, this scripture presents Lucifer s declaration that he would ascend into heaven and take the place of the highest God. He desired to exalt his throne above the stars of God; to sit upon the mount of the congregation and in doing all this, He would be like God.

God heard all of these boastings, and He responded by decreeing that Lucifer would be thrown into hell and would become a spectacle; he would be mocked and scorned, cast out of his grave like a carcass and that he would be alone.

These statements were made in heaven during what is known as the anti-chaotic period or the dispensation of angels. God gave angels rulership to administer His will and to rule the earth. At that time, angels were sinless and that included Lucifer. He was the ruling cherub of the earth and was described as:

Perfect in thy ways from the day that thou was created, till iniquity was found in thee. EZEKIEL 28:11- 17

These two scriptures tell us that satan had a favourable beginning. He was placed in a perfect situation and could have remained in that position until this day, had he not been taken in pride, and wanted to dethrone God.

I can just imagine God saying to Lucifer:

Lucifer, I have made you perfect and I ve placed you in a perfect situation. All around you is perfection, but that is not enough for you. I see that what you want is a fight so a fight you are going to get.

God did not have to hold a long battle with Lucifer, after-all what was there to fight with? You cannot fight with someone who has created you, because there is no questioning the fact that the tactics of your creator must exceed yours. This demonstrates just how silly satan is.

Lucifer wanted to fight against his mastermind. I am sure that the Lord must have just calmly pointed a finger at him and asked him to get out with those angels that had rebelled. How could Lucifer think that he could be equal to our Lord let alone be greater than Him?

He had lost this battle in heaven and was cast out, and his name was changed to satan. He lost at Eden when he expected that he would be able to befriend the woman, Eve, but instead God placed enmity between them and sent him crawling away on his stomach. He tried to use Herod to kill Jesus at His birth, and that also did not take off.

He has a way of waiting for an opportune moment in which to pounce. You see he is like a roaring Lion. This is why he waited for Jesus in the wilderness after His long period of fasting, because satan knew that after 40 days the Lord s flesh would have been very weak. Satan does not even know that fasting decreases the flesh but increases the spirit and so when he tempted Jesus he was again defeated. Jesus would have been weak in the flesh but strong in the spirit.

However, as we know, this serpent is very cunning and will not just go when he is rebuked. He will disappear for a while to listen to and to study your plans and to see how best he can set you up. Nevertheless, as we all know, He has no fighting tactics and no winning strategy. Therefore, having been defeated in the wilderness, he waited for Jesus at Calvary and that was where he got his greatest whipping and lost both rulership of the earth, and the keys to hell. He is always a loser but he continues to fight.

Moreover, his worst whipping is yet to come because he is gone to wait at the battle of the Armageddon and that is where his end will truly come. For the Lord will not be defeated by what he has created.

DEVILS VERSUS DEMONS

I have read many books, which have given the same explanation for devil and demon. There is only one devil and this devil, satan, controls demons who carry out his wicked schemes. The Greek word **diabolos** meaning an accuser or slanderer is one of the names of satan. The English word devil is derived from this and should be only used to describe him.

Daimon on the other hand, which is frequently used for devil, means demon in English. The scripture does not give us any description of the origin of demons. However, we do have several biblical testimonies of their existence and activities. They are presented as disembodied spirits, which enter the bodies of people and take up their abode in them Mark 16:9 and Luke 8: 2, shows this.

Their victims generally show signs of madness, epilepsy, depression, panic attack, and other illnesses, which are associated with the nervous system. Person/s who are under the influence of these evil spirits will quite often lose their self control, show multiply personalities, have different voices speaking through them, and have these wicked beings taking them from place to place. Sometimes these victims show supernatural strength.

Other demon spirits will enter the bodies of their victims and speak through them as clairvoyants, mediums, fortune-tellers, or witches. Many of these people will either have acquired a generational curse, or have been a victim of the evil one, while others would have voluntarily made pacts with the devil to enthral these demons in exchange for wealth and fame in the form of covenanting. Their ends are generally disastrous. Accounts will be given later in this volume of true-life experience.

A person who is possessed with a demon has to go through a process, which is called deliverance. This is the English equivalent to the Greek word **rhuomai**, which means to rescue from , to preserve from , and so to deliver. It is synonymous with **sozo**, which means to save. In essence, a person who is possessed with a demon has to be saved from that spirit. This person is therefore in a very dangerous position and can eventually die if s/he is not rescued.

Many church leaders seem to be quite wary of the many deliverance ministries that are now springing up around the world, and although some prudence is wise, we must realise that spiritual warfare has been a living reality since the beginning of time. The Bible tells us that as it was in the beginning so will it be in the end and the Bible cannot lie.

We see the whole creation story being centred around three characters - God, satan and Man. God created man and placed him in a perfect situation. Satan then deceived man and became a Pseudo-god of the universe. God s intention therefore is to make the earth as it was before the fall of man.

On the other hand, satan s ultimate objective is to hang on to the universe, because he wants to be the owner. The earth began with a war in heaven for rulership. Satan wanted to become ruler, and today this is still his intention.

I believe that as we draw closer to the fulfilment of the Bible, we will find satan letting loose more of his dark forces. These will undoubtedly inhabit the lives of those who are vulnerable, and will result in a lot of confusion amongst people and nations. I believe that this will be his last onslaught and that he is secretly gathering his horde of darkness.

In my spirit, I can see a whole gang of territorial spirits hanging over various nations and they are preparing to create confusion amongst these territories. As Christians, it is our responsibility to go into intensive prayer and fasting so as to defeat them. I cannot see the wise and all-knowing God that we serve being quite happy to sit back, relax and watch satan as he gather his army for war.

Our God is too sagacious for that. Satan will never have rulership of this earth and our Lord is now ensuring that while satan is gathering his army, The Lord is gathering His as well. THERE IS GOING TO BE AN END TIME WAR!

The Lord is telling His Churches to Prepare for war . If we be fooled and sit still without putting on our armour, then the churches will be in trouble, and will surely be defeated in this end time.

PREPARING FOR WAR

On the same day when evening had come. He said to them. Let us cross over to the other side Now when they had sent away the multitude, they took Him even as He was in the ship. And other little ships were also with Him.

And a great windstorm arose, and the waves beat into the ship, so that it was already filling. But he was in the stern asleep on a pillow. And they awoke Him and said to Him, Teacher do you not care that we are perishing?

Then He awoke and He rebuked the wind and said to the storm Peace be still! And the wind ceased and there was a great calm. Mark 4:35-39.

Whenever the Lord has a great plan for your life, the devil has a way of stepping in to create a great storm. His idea is to see if he can get you off course. However, I am confident that the greater the battle that you are faced with, the greater the glory which the Lord receives. In addition, the greater the victory is, the greater the blessings that are laid up for you.

satan is just a bully who has neither fighting tactics nor winning strategies. He knows how to create a storm, but only you can allow him to get the victory out of that storm. He reminds me of the cowards who usually use fear to manipulate his weaker opponents.

Don t tell or I will kill you.
Give me your money or I ll get my friends to beat you up.

If you refuse to marry me then I will murder myself.

Do not listen to them, for if you do, eventually you will become just like them. The moment you begin to stand up to bullies and to show them that you are not a defeatist, the sooner they will learn to back off and to leave you alone. If you never challenge bullies they will forever challenge you.

In the above text, we have the picture of Jesus on His way to Gadarene, where He had a great work to perform in that He had some nasty spirits to deal with. These demons had been comfortably living in the Gadarene man for a long time. They were carrying out the plans of their master. He had found a snug home for them and when they vacated that property, their master would have had the responsibility of rehousing them.

In the same chapter we are told that the demons asked to be sent into pigs, but we also learned that they were destroyed as the pigs had to drown themselves, because they can t swim.

Jesus was about to create a stir in Gadare, and we can only imagine what this miracle did to the people living there. Their lives would have been changed forever. Even those who did not believe in the Lord would surely say:

Of a truth, this is the Son of God.

We understand then, that satan did not want Jesus to go to Gadare, so much that he created a great storm on the sea. The word great is taken from the Greek root word **mega** and is generally used to describe something of gigantic proportions. Here we have a mighty windstorm, and this was intended to cause the boat to capsize, or for Jesus to change His course.

However no one knows the schemes and devices of satan more than the Lord, who rebuked the storm and even the wind and the sea had to obey Him. So great is the God that we serve, a God who knows when the winds of our lives are about to sweep us off shore.

A God who knows when the Problems in our lives seem so gigantic that we feel that on our own we cannot deal with them. A God, who knows our divine purposes and knows when to command mountains to get out of our way so that His purpose will be fulfilled in our lives.

Our God will not let us down but we on the other hand must submit our ways to Him. For if the enemy can try to dissuade the Lord from fulfilling His purpose, then who are we for him not to want to do the same thing to? Therefore as children of God, we must be fully armoured to deal with demons.

When the Lord called me, He had a mega task for me to perform. The devil also knew that the Lord had this plan for my life and so he tried to kill me before I could get to fulfil the purpose for my life. However God has a way of turning every negative thing that happens in your life around for good. And so while he was trying to destroy my life, the Lord was bringing me to another level.

He was taking me into a perfect relationship with Him and to a place where I could receive power with authority to command demons to go in the name of Jesus. He was taking me to a place where I could take a stand against spiritual wickedness in high places, against principalities, against powers, and against the rulers of the darkness of this world.

The Lord stripped me of a corruptible robe, He took me to the refiner s pot, and like gold he tried me just as described by Malachi:

The Lord is like a refiner s fire and like launderer s soap He will sit as a refiner and a purifier of silver. MALACHI 3:2 - 3

The word refine is derived from the Hebrew word **puroomai**, which means to be burned and to be tried. The Lord tried me through that period of illness and He spiritually burned those satanic dregs out of my life.

DEVILS CANNOT CAST OUT DEVILS

Then certain of the vagabond Jews, exorcists, took upon them to call over them which had evil spirits the name of the Lord Jesus saying: We adjure you by Jesus whom Paul preacheth.

And there were seven sons of Sceva, a Jew, and chief priests, which did so. And the evil spirit answered and said Jesus I know, and Paul I know, but who are ye?

And the man in whom the evil spirit was leaped on them and overcame them and prevailed against them so that they fled out of that house naked and wounded. ACTS 19:13—16.

We have to know in whose name and by what means we are casting out demons, because these are very wicked and vicious spirits. If we are unprepared when we come to face them, they will kill us. They will turn upon you just as they did to the men of Sceva. It takes a spiritually prepared person to cast out demons, not just a person who knows how to call on the name of Jesus, but instead a blood washed child of God. In addition, the Lord has a way of allowing a blood washed child of God to understand the tactics of the evil ones before calling him to such a ministry.

To become a deliverance minister, the child of God has to be like the refiner s gold. He has to be taken repeatedly to the refiner s pot and be purged and purged until the full glory of the Lord shines from within him. Therefore, the first step is to be thoroughly cleansed from within, and the key teachings for spiritual cleansing can be found in the book of Ephesians. This epistle contains some rather solid teachings on spiritual warfare.

Although some theologians might say that this epistle was written to all the churches, many have overlooked the fact that this particular church in Ephesus was under demonic attack. I believe that Paul needed to explain to them why although they were professing to be born again children of God they were under such attack.

Therefore, he began to teach them as to how they should adorn themselves from within. Paul was well aware that spiritual warfare begins from within and that if the mind is not clean from all corruption that it will become the ideal battle ground for the enemy. One just cannot cast out demons with an unclean mind. Demons love dirt.

Let us look at some of the names for the lord of the demons.

The apostle Paul, in writing to the church at Corinth asked them the question:

On what accord has Christ with Belial?

Belial is only one of the many names for satan and in Hebrew, this has two meanings as given by Vine.

The first is that it means worthlessness, unprofitable or wickedness, while the secondary meaning is destruction. Another meaning is abode of the dead. In the quote above, it means the destroyer. It is also related to **Beliar**, which means Lord of the forest .

Beelzebub is another name for satan, which in Hebrew means Lord of the flies , as found in 2 Kings 1:2. The name was later changed in Greek to **Beelzabub**, meaning Lord of the dunghill , as found in St Matthew 12:24, and later **Baalzebul**, to mean Lord of abominable idols and idolatry, the worst and chief of all wickedness. St Matthew 10:25.

He is called a dragon in Revelation 12 and in 1Timothy 5:14, he is called our adversary . He is the devil in St Matthew 4 and Ephesians 6. He is called a thief in John 10, a serpent in Revelation 12, and an accuser of the brethren in the same chapter. He is prince of the powers of the air in Ephesians 6. He is our enemy in St Matthew 13, god of this world in 2 Corinthians 2 and prince of the world in St John 12.

All of these names explain to us that this devil is a very nasty and evil serpent and that no one should want to play with him. The apostle Peter tells us in 1Peter that we should:

be sober, and be vigilant; because our adversary the devil walketh about, seeking whom he may devour. 1 PETER

The Greek word for adversary is **antikidos**. It is used, to refer a lawsuit and also as without reference to legal affairs. I think that in both senses here, as the devil accuses men before God on a daily basis just as he did to Job.

Therefore, we know that we have an adversary, whose evil eyes are always watching us to see if we will make any mistakes that would give him legal grounds to destroy our lives. Therefore, we ought to be sober. The Greek word for sober as used in this verse is **nepho** and it means to be free from the influence of intoxication. It is also used to mean watch. The word vigilant is used in the sense of the Greek word **gregoreo**, and means to be awake, never be off your guard, to be ready every moment to resist the devil.

Peter is not saying that you should always be consumed with thoughts of the devil. Instead, he is reminding us that we have an enemy who is so mad with us that he is treating us as an opponent in a lawsuit. He is in fact taking us to a daily court and therefore we should be aware of his existence and his tactics. We must be on the guard.

To be on guard here does not mean to keep your eyes open. What it means is that we should be spiritually prepared at all times lest he catches us off guard. So how do we stay spiritually on guard? The apostle Paul demonstrates this to us once again in the book of Ephesians. I find this writing very fitting not only for every child of God, but more so for those who are in the deliverance Ministry.

A SPIRITUAL DRESS-UP

For the weapons of our warfare are not carnal, but mighty through God to the pulling down of strongholds. Casting down imaginations, and every high thing that exalteth itself against the knowledge of God, and bringing into captivity every thought to the obedience of Christ. 2 CORINTHIANS 10:4-5.

Paul was preparing the church at Ephesus for spiritual warfare. He is showing us that we have spiritual weapons that are not carnal. However, we need to prepare ourselves before we can use those weapons, otherwise they will be ineffective. Remember that this is a spiritual battle and not a physical one, so we should not expect to use ordinary weapons in this fight.

...aking to this church firstly turned his spiritual torch within. He looks ...mind of the believers. An unclean mind is the perfect breeding ground for ...mons and Jesus just will not share house with the devil. Moreover, if your spirit is not clean then you will not be able to handle spiritual weapons. We are advised here to dress ourselves righteously from within, and to cleanse ourselves from all filthiness.

If you were living an ungodly life, and you were trying to cast out demons, then you should be very careful, as they will turn on you just as they did to the seven sons of Sceva. The devil knows you and what you are about. Remember what they said to the exorcists?

Jesus I know and Paul I know, but who are you?

Being a churchgoer alone does not give you authority to cast out demons; it takes a blood washed person to do so.

If you review my earlier testimony, you will recall that when I was praying for my deliverance, I was directed to the book of James chapter 5 and verse 16,

The effectual fervent prayer of a righteous man availeth much.

Please take particular note of the word righteous , which is derived from the Greek word **dikaiosune** meaning the quality of being just, having the attributes of Christ and to be Christ like. It also means to be truthful and also to be faithful, to be obedient, to become in Christ all that God requires a man to be, and all that a man could never be in himself. It means walking uprightly, and being able to exercise faith.

This is the only type of person that I felt could deliver me from the plans of the enemy, and, I began to pray that the Lord would send me someone with such qualities. When those persons came they were able to cast those stubborn demons out because they were walking in righteousness.

WALKING IN RIGHTEOUSNESS

How then does one walk in righteousness? Firstly, Paul reminds us in Ephesians 4 that we have been redeemed through the blood of Jesus and that our sins have been forgiven.

As children of God, there are times when the accuser of the brethren, will try to tell us that we are not saved. Well if he does not have any secrets for you, then you are saved.

If you have confessed your sins, been baptised, filled with the Holy Ghost and are living a godly life then you are saved. Paul further reminds us of our past, present and future. He said that we were once dead in trespasses and sin.

We used to walk according to the course of this world, according to the prince of the power of the air. He also says that we once conducted ourselves in the lusts of the flesh, fulfilling the desires of the flesh, and the mind, and that we were children of wrath. We are now alive through grace, and we are seated in heavenly places in Christ Jesus.

Furthermore He says that we were Gentiles in the flesh and that we were without Christ. We were once a far off, but now are brought near by the blood of Christ. We are told that we have peace in Christ and therefore we should walk worthy, with lowliness of spirit, we should be gentle, with longsuffering. We should bear with one another. Keep the unity of the spirit in the bond of peace.

In the same chapter, we are told to put away lying, that we can be angry but that we should not sin. We must not grieve the Holy Spirit within us. We should not steal, we should not give ourselves over to lewdness or to do unclean work, and we should not be greedy. We as born again Christians, have put off the corrupt old man and are now renewed in the spirit by putting on the new man, which is Christ Jesus.

We must be careful what we say. We should avoid corrupt communications. We must say things that are edifying. We must put away bitterness, wrath, anger, clamour, and malice.

We are told that we should be kind one to another, be tender hearted and forgiving.

In chapter five of the same book of Ephesians, we are encouraged to walk in love, as Christ loves us. We are told that we should avoid fornication, all uncleanness or covetousness, filthiness, foolish talking or coarse jesting. We are further reminded that we were once in darkness but that we are now light in the Lord and that we should walk as children of light.

We should have no fellowship with the unfruitful works of darkness but we should instead expose them. We should walk in wisdom, and should avoid drinking strong drink to excess. Paul further went on to give counselling to married partners, to parents and also to children.

For us to be able to walk in righteousness then, we would need to pay attention to all of the above teachings. It is only by observing those teachings and by practising them that we are in a position to engage the enemy.

As pointed out before, filth just cannot fight with filth. You cannot fight with the enemy unless you are prepared from within to do so. Sin is an open doorway for the enemy, and if we are living in sin and should try to engage in spiritual warfare, then we would only be inviting the enemy in through our open sinful doors. This can only be dangerous for us, because we would be turned upon and be beaten just as the sons of Sceva were beaten.

I have read many books in which the writers have gone into details to explain how we should engage the enemy without looking at the quality of life that the believer is living. They have talked at length about the offensive and defensive weapons that are available. Many of these writers tend to give the impression that anyone can use these weapons. However, although these weapons are available to everyone, not everyone has the authority to use them. You must be walking in holiness to be able to take authority over the kingdom of darkness.

Paul was saying to the church in Ephesus, and to all in the body of Jesus Christ.

Search yourself to see whether or not you are living a holy and a righteous life before engaging in spiritual warfare.

He is pointing out to us that if we are operating in any of the sins that have been outlined above then we need to rid ourselves of them and get dressed in righteousness. When we are dressed in righteousness from within the devil will have no legal grounds on which to invade our lives.

When it was time for me to be delivered from the evil one, the demons could not put up a fight because already I was learning how to walk in holiness. I had surrendered my life to the Lord and although I had no one to teach me how to walk with Christ, I would pick up my Bible daily and allow the Lord to guide me into studying the passages that would assist me in this Christian walk.

When I went to the occultists, they could not help me as they were living in darkness and darkness just cannot overcome light. It is the light that overcomes the darkness, however as the devil works in darkness his fruits are unfruitful. Demons just will not cast out demons, rather, their intention is to attract other demons to join them.

Clearly deliverance is a two-fold thing, firstly the person who is conducting the deliverance should be prepared, but in addition the demonised should be prepared. We will elaborate on preparing a person for deliverance in later chapters.

Sin causes the weapons of our warfare to feel heavy in our hands. We hold the sword but it becomes too heavy for us to swing around. We are wearing the armour, but we cannot walk in them because they are too heavy. We have the shoes on our feet but we cannot move in them, we cannot lift our feet because sin is holding them to the ground.

Having cleansed ourselves we now have access to those weapons of our warfare, which are not carnal, but are mighty through God to the pulling down of strongholds. We can now put those weapons into their rightful places and begin to use them effectively and with the authority that only comes from being a blood washed Child of God.

Chapter 10

Covered by The Blood

Finally my brethren be strong in the Lord and in the power of His might. Put on the whole armour of God that ye may be able to stand against the wiles of the devil. For we wrestle not against flesh and blood, but against principalities, against powers, against the rulers of the darkness of this world, against spiritual hosts of wickedness in the heavenly places. Therefore take up the whole armour of God that you may be able to withstand in the evil day, and having done all to stand. Stand therefore having your loins girt with truth, having put on the breastplate of righteousness. And having shod your feet with the preparation of the gospel of peace. Above all taking the shield of faith with which you will be able to quench all the fiery darts of the wicked one. And take the helmet of salvation and the sword of the spirit, which is the word of God. Praying always with all prayer and supplication in the spirit, being watchful to this end with all perseverance and supplication for all the saints. Ephesians 6:10-18

SATAN S HIERARCHY

We understand from these verses that the devil has structured his evil spirits, and has placed them in hierarchical positions. I know from my own experiences with the kingdom of darkness that these demon spirits will attack you according to your station with the Lord, and also according to the calling that He has placed upon your life.

I am also aware that they know the strength of your spiritual weapons. Although we can pretend to man that we are seated in heavenly places with Christ Jesus, far above principalities and powers, we just cannot fool these unclean spirits because the Bible tells us clearly that we will have to pass through their dwelling place to reach to the third heaven where Christ reigns (Ephesians. 2:6).

I would like to draw reference from my own experience to explain this. I believe that when the devil decided to destroy my life, he had what I would call a conference in hell. I believe that first he called up his principalities and powers. He would have told them of the plan to destroy my life and would have also sat with them to work out the best way in which to accomplish this.

Having arrived at their wicked scheme, I think that they would then have delegated the responsibility for my destruction further down the rank to the rulers of the darkness of this world, who would then draw demon spirits from the rank of spiritual wickedness in high places to attack me directly. I believe that they had not planned for a fight. I was supposed to be easy prey as I was in their kingdom and was walking according to the course of the prince of this world.

When they came in, to their disdain, the spirit of the Lord came in and set up a standard against them, and on returning to satan with reports of a failed mission, he then assigned the hosts of wickedness to do the job themselves.

When that failed he assigned the rulers of the darkness of this age to the task, and when they failed, he got his principalities and powers on the job, after which he personally began to do his visitations. He is not God and therefore he is not omnipotent, omniscient or omnipresent. Therefore, he has to assign his demons to carry out his evil work.

I am sure that if I had been living a clean and righteous life style, they would not have been able to attack me unless God had given them permission to do so, as in the case of Job.

Paul is advising us that there are various ranks of demon spirits that are set against us, that they are well organised and that these are very wicked and malicious forces. We are being given a sound word of advice however, in that we are advised to put on the whole armour of God.

This is a final word of precaution that Paul is giving to us. He has gone to great lengths to teach us about sound Christian living; the foremost thing that we need before even thinking about spiritual warfare.

Paul concludes the epistle by using the word Finally . He uses this word a lot in ending his epistles. In each of these epistles, he gives his sound teachings, but he has a way of leaving something that is very important for the end or the background on which the whole epistle is based.

He uses the word Finally from the Greek root **loipon** meaning for the rest of the matter , or in conclusion . Paul is saying here:

I have laid before you your high calling and the great doctrine of the gospel. In addition to that I have also shown you how to walk in righteousness. Now that I feel that you are ready to engage your enemies, I will now show you how they will oppose you and how you need to overcome them.

First, he says that you must be strong in the Lord. He is not referring to the lion s strength, or the strength of Samson. He is referring to that of little David, and the strength that accompanies faith in the Lord, the **endunamoo** strength [Greek].

This strength lies in your weapon. It lies in the armour of God. Therefore he says that you should put on the whole armour of God.

With our armour in place, we will be able to stand in the strength of David, in the strength of Joshua, in that of Gideon and also in that of Jehosaphath.

THE ARMOUR OF GOD

Now Paul says:

   put on the whole armour of God, that ye may be able to stand against the wiles of the devil.

There are four words that I would like us to look at in this sentence. The first word, whole as used in this verse, is derived from the Greek word '**Holokleros**', meaning entire, and armour is from the word '**panoplia**', referring to the full armour of a heavily armed soldier. Stand is from the word **Histemi**, meaning by your faith, and of steadfastness. Finally, the word wiles is used from the Greek root, **Methodia** meaning a cunning device. It denotes craft, deceit, or to lie in wait to deceive.

This passage is therefore telling us that the devil is very sly and cunning. Also that he will use cunning devices to catch us, and therefore we should be spiritually dressed throughout and stand in steadfastness and in faith against him.

The soldier going to war knows that he must be dressed in the appropriate war attire otherwise he will expose himself to danger. His first and foremost responsibility is to prepare himself for battle and that is to be dressed in his defensive armour. He further needs to have his offensive gear in place, and so he must have a prepared mind. He knows that he is not going on the battlefield to lose the fight, so he has to get himself mentally, psychologically and emotionally prepared.

Have you ever looked at the face of a soldier in war on your television screen? You would sometimes wonder if he has any thoughts of death in his mind. He appears to be so resolute. If you were to have a look at the guards on duty, at Westminster or at Buckingham Palace, you would notice how firmly they stand their grounds. They have a job to do which carries a mandate that they stand, and they will neither look to the left nor to the right, they are on duty and so they stand.

As a deliverance minister and one who is coming against the cunning schemes of the devil, Paul is telling us not to be intimidated by the devil s cowardly, crafty and cunning schemes. Stand your ground against the enemy; stand against him in faith and on the word of God. You have the authority because you are more than a conqueror.

We are also being given a very strong piece of advice here.

"For we wrestle not against flesh and blood.

This sentence carries a similar message to that of 2 Corinthians 10:4.

"For the weapons of our warfare are not carnal, but mighty through God to the pulling down of stronghold.

I remember using many carnal weapons when I was under spiritual attack. Occultic oils and incense, candles, washes and perfumes to name a few. None of them worked, and, in fact, they were the perfect attraction for these demon spirits because those are some of their very own dirty weapons. By using those things I was only sending an open invitation to them.

This is also a warning to those people who say that they are in the Lord but have incense burning in their homes, have little talismans and other charms on them, have been visiting occultists for little portions to drink and are wearing all types of guard rings and chains. I am warning you that these are very dangerous occultic tools and I will speak at length on those things later.

There were times when I would have used those things and shortly after using them would actually feel a heavy oppression building up around the house. I was sending an open requisition to satan and his hosts of hell. Those were effectively, carnal weapons.

At the time of writing this book, I was in my sleep when I sensed the presence of evil in my house. The presumptuousness of the enemy greatly upset me. I was immediately awake and felt like jumping out of bed to physically chase them out. However, I heard the Lord gently said to me:

 Remember Lona, the weapons of your warfare are not carnal, but they are mighty.

With that assurance, I just pointed my finger to the door and calmly declared:
I order you out in the name of Jesus.

They left because they had to respond to weapons that are authoritatively used in the name of Jesus. If I were a spiritual coward, who would have got up and cried without taking authority over them, then they would have created havoc in my home. But I live in a blood washed home and I give no room to evil spirits in my life. I am under the blood of Jesus.

But against principalities, against powers, against the rulers of the darkness of this world. Against spiritual wickedness in high places.

Paul places these demon rebels into rank, in a descending order according to their status with satan. At the very top he places the principalities. The Greek word for principality is arche and has to do with rulers, and governments and signifies the authoritative position of fallen angels.

These principalities therefore, form the rank of the governing or ruling demons that discharge instructions on behalf of their leader. They obviously form the highest order.

Next in rank we have the powers. This is derived from the word exousiazo, which means to exercise authority. Examining the hierarchy, it is apparent that the principalities pass on instruction to the powers; the powers then delegate these responsibilities to the rulers of the darkness of this world, that is, kosmokratopas, meaning rulers of the cosmos. These therefore are the high-ranking demons that occupy the cosmos.

Finally we have, spiritual wickedness in high places. This is from another Greek word, which is 'pneumatika ponerias', and relates to the wicked spirits of satan that abide in the heavenlies. These two last groups form the lower ranks, and generally take directives from the higher groups. They are the ones who directly execute the plans and devices of satan.

We now know that not only is the devil very evil and wicked, but that he also has structured evil spirits that carry out his dirty works. We also know that they are highly organised and that we cannot just approach them anyhow. We too must be organised, and we must be in a position to execute our structured plans against him, just as he is doing against us.

God is our commander — in — charge who has a force behind Him which is better trained, more equipped, more resilient, much more organised and forms a greater force than that of the enemy. However, God will not assign His angels to work for us if we are not living a holy life.

He says be ye holy for I am holy . God cannot bear to look at sin; consequently if we want the Lord to help us then we must obey Him. This is the only way to be assured that there will be no battle that is too hard for Him to fight for you.

I never knew the magnitude of what I was engaged in, nor was I prepared for such attack. When it happened I was exposed, and I had no protective clothing. As a result, the enemies were able to hit me really hard. It is only through the grace of God that I am here today, and therefore I am warning you that if you are out there playing with the devil, to get out of his camp as fast as you can because you are treading on dangerous ground.

He is a liar and the father of it says the Lord in the book of John. The devil is a con man. He will trick you into believing that he can give you anything that you want, and to allow you to feel secure in him. He is like a fox that is only luring you into his den. As soon as he has lured you in completely, he will begin to laugh nastily in your face. His plan is to destroy you. He is so evil and heartless that he lies in wait and pounces on you in your hours of greatest need.

It is however such peace to know that our God is a God of the bad times and a God of the good times, He is a God of the mountains and a God of the valley, a God of the night and a God of the day. All we need to do is put our trust in him. If the Lord had not put his armour around me, then I know that I just would not be here today. To God be the Glory!

Paul continues to instruct us as to the preparation that we will need to make, so as to be able to engage the spiritual forces of darkness that are assigned against us. He says that once we have our armours on and we are wearing them in their rightful places, and when we know that we are dressed in holiness from within, then we should not run away from the enemy. He is saying that we should stand and confront him. The word stand has been used three times in these verses to emphasise the importance of having confidence in the Lord to fight our battles.

Once you have the Lord dwelling in you, then be assured that He will bring you to a place of security, where He will assign battalions of angels to watch over you and the gates of hell will not be able to prevail against you.

I remember one night having cast some demons out of a young man, who had those forces with him from he was born. His condition also reminded me of that of the woman with the issue of blood.

This young man confessed that he had been to every known occultists, looking for help. He said that he was only directed to me when he had spent all that he had. When he came that day, he had demons looking at me through his eyes. He was so confused that he didn t know himself. That night we took authority and got rid of those evils, and the young man accepted the Lord.

In the dead of the night, the lights went out. I woke up just as they were going out. I found the incident very peculiar as I had never seen electricity shut off like that in London. I looked across to the houses nearby and they too had no electric current. I then fumbled with my phone in the dark and called the electricity board.

Oh they told me, we have been informed that something strange is happening at Brunswick Court. I quietly sat down and began to pray. Suddenly I had a vision of trembling demons returning to satan and they were saying to him: we can t go there, that place is covered by the blood of Jesus.
We sat in peace and confidence, knowing that:

The weapons of our warfare were not carnal but that they were mighty through God to the pulling down of strongholds.

We were not just a conquering force, but that we were more than conquerors. God is calling forth deliverance ministers who are not afraid, who are always confident that they that are with them are always more than those that are against them. Folks who know that once they are enrolled in the army of Jesus Christ then they needn t be afraid because they have some big brothers who form the heavenly troops, and who are always armoured with some spiritual guerrilla bombs to drop in the enemy s camp.

In these verses the apostle has given us all the weapons that we need to fight against the enemy. He says that you should stand having your loins girt about with truth. That is having the word of God with you, which you can throw at the devil when the occasion arises.

The Lord says in His word that though heaven and earth may pass away, none of His words ever would. In the book of Isaiah, the prophet Isaiah tells us that:

So shall they that fear the Lord from the west, and His glory from the rising of the sun. When the enemy shall come in like a flood, the spirit of the Lord shall set up a standard against him. ISAIAH 59:19

In Christ we know that:

no weapon that is formed against us shall prosper, and that any tongue that rises up against us in judgement shall be condemned. ISAIAH 54:17

When we have this truth within our spirits, accompanied by righteous living, then the enemy knows that he has no place in our lives.

Paul further reminds us of the importance of trusting in God and of having faith in Him.

PREPARING YOURSELF FOR DELIVERANCE

In earlier chapters I have reviewed briefly the methods I used to develop faith in the Lord to deliver me from the evil one. In the first instance I was looking for help everywhere except from the Lord. When those attempts failed I was faced with either of two choices. I was either going to die or turn to Jesus. I chose the Lord.

When I was coming out of the world I had a small measure of faith. It was the weakness in this area of faith that would have failed me. However, as I began to study the words of God, my faith began to grow. It was this that allowed those righteous people of God to come to my help. It was trough faith that they were on prayer and fasting when they came, and it was by faith that those demons had to leave my body. I am also sure that those praying people had faith in the Lord to deliver me when they came.

During that period, I had also developed a prayerful lifestyle. It was prayer that led me to Matthew chapter 17, and to realise that I could only be delivered through prayer and fasting.

God in His own way was also training me to become a solid deliverance minister. It is my experience, which has led me to this branch of ministry. Through that suffering, I had developed sympathy and love for folks who are under siege by the evil one.

My past experiences with occultism have allowed me grave insights into the tactics used by the prince of darkness. They have also enabled me to identify his schemes and devices. When the devil had me in his camp, he did not know that he was helping to train me to become a great disciple of Jesus Christ. Today I know that he is still holding at ransom many of God s wonderful end time ministers who I pray will one day be released from his slave market.

As mentioned earlier, the devil has no winning tactics, nor does he have fighting strategies. For one day God is going break those prison doors open, and He will set those prisoners free. Those same people that are being held at ransom will be rising up against the devil and will give God the glory.

Chapter 11

Steps to Deliverance

Then He called His disciples together and gave them power and authority over all devils and to cure diseases and He sent them to preach the kingdom of God and to heal the sick' Luke 9: 1-2

STEP ONE: LIVING A RIGHTEOUS LIFE

In this chapter we will review the preparation, which was undertaken by the deliverance team who offered me deliverance and then try to match those with the teachings of Ephesians.

The principal message of Paul in his letter to the Ephesians, in essence, was the acknowledgement that the church had a vicious enemy to fight and that in order for them to stand against that enemy they needed to be prepared. He then explained that this preparation begins from within, that is, from the spirit man.

We are all aware as Christians that the mind is the devil s central battle ground, and that we would certainly be in trouble if we attempted to confront the enemy without preparing our spirit man.

This is not a physical battle and we are not fighting with flesh and blood. In other words, we are not at war with a human being against whom we can use physical guns, spears or machetes. We are fighting with a great force of unseen spirit beings that are very nasty, and that respond positively to a sinful nature.

They can quickly identify a soul that has not been crucified and one that has not been submitted to the will of God and as such these are precisely the souls that they will fight with and successfully usurp.

However, when we have a surrendered soul, a crucified body and a spirit that is submitted to the will, word, and obedience of God, the devil has no open doors through which to enter and to destroy our lives. This is why Paul encourages us to clean up our lives and to lay all our cares on the altar of sacrifice. When we do this, then we are assured that when the enemy comes in :

like a flood, the Spirit of the Lord will step in and will set up a standard against him .

What a beautiful assurance!

To some people this can seem impossible. This is because the enemy is still holding their minds captive. The Lord, however, reminds us in the book of John that:

the thief cometh not but to steal and to kill, and to destroy.

But that:

He has come that we might have life, and that we might have it more abundantly.

He also says that:

He is the good shepherd and the good shepherd giveth his life for his sheep
John 10:10 — 11

Can you imagine a thief giving his life for you? Satan would never give up anything for you; instead he will use you and then make a dirty sacrifice of you. As far as he is concerned you are finished with, and he has no more use for you.

We thank God that he is a being that specialises in finished products. God will always take you from wherever you are, and make you into someone that is more than you ever thought you could be.

Have you ever noticed that the end product is always the best and richest? When I was a child growing up in the Jamaica, I can still remember going to the sugar mill to collect the sweet molasses. This was the end product of the cane after the sugar has been extracted. However, this was the most delicious part, the waste product.

What the enemy does not know is that should you return to the Lord when he is finished with you, if you reach out for the Lord when you have become the end product that he thinks is good for nothing, he would no longer have any hold over you. Having been so far down his road there would be nothing left that he would be able to entice you with.

He has shown you all and you have learnt his tactics. When you turn your life over to Jesus, God will turn your situation around and make the best disciple of you. When Satan conspired to crucify the Lord he thought that his death would be the end of Him.

I can imagine him sitting around his conference table in hell with his hordes of principalities and powers, making ready to celebrate the death of the crucified Lord. Just imagine the horrified look on the faces of those demons as Jesus descended into their midst, made an open show of the devil and snatched the keys of hell out of his evil hands!

Just when the enemy thought that it was finished, the Lord was saying:

No! This is not the end; this is the beginning of man s redemption. I have just given my blood for the redemption of man. Now they can have life everlasting. You will not be able to hold the souls of the righteous in hell anymore Satan. My people are no more in your slave market they are now redeemed, not by gold or silver but by my precious blood!

Satan had lost again and he still has a final battle to lose. He is well aware of this and this is precisely why he is in a hurry to destroy your soul.

You, therefore, should be in a hurry to make it right with the Lord. The people who came to deliver me had salvation buried within their souls. I did not know them at all, but one thing I did know is that those demons obeyed them and left my body immediately. Those people came with power and authority. They were living a righteous life and as such they had access to the throne of grace. They were seated in heavenly places with Christ Jesus.

If we take the example of the great apostle Paul, who was a persecutor of the churches, we will see that although he was working for the devil and had succeeded in destroying so many Christians, yet when he found the goodness of the Lord he became the best apostle in biblical record.

Satan specialises in filth and uncleanness, but our God is a God of purity. He is a God of righteousness, a God of honesty, love, mercy and compassion. Therefore, in order to fight against the enemy, we should not be wearing clothes, which are similar to those in which he is dressed, but rather in similar clothing to that of the Lord.

Ours should be of a superior quality. In fact, we should be robed in righteousness, so that when we speak to demons they have no choice but to obey us.

Consequently, your first step in spiritual warfare is to make sure that you are living a clean and a pure life. You must be sure that the sinful nature does not reign in you, that you have the Holy Ghost living inside of you and that you have made the Lord Jesus Christ Lord of your life.

Your strength does not lie in shouting at the devil; some shouts are very empty and will only wear you out. We can recall the backsliding Israelites who were at war with the Philistines (1Samuel ch.4) who, having lost a first battle consulted with the Lord as to whether or not they would have won this impending one. When they did not get any reply, they went before the ark of the Lord shouting.

The Israelites shouted and the walls of Jericho came down. They shouted and the Hittites, Ammonites and Jebusites were destroyed under Jehosaphat, they shouted at the battle of Gideon and the invading armies were defeated. They now felt that though they had backslidden they could come into the presence of the Lord, and shout Him out of the Holy of the Holiest.

However, their shouting was to no avail because the presence of the Lord had departed from them, and consequently the Philistines captured the Ark of the Covenant from them when in fact it should never have fallen out of the hands of the house of Israel.

Suffice to say, the Lord will not respond to an empty shout. We cannot shout demons out of anyone if we are not living a holy life. Our strength lies in our salvation.

A person who is strong in the Lord is one who dwells in the secret place of the most high, and abides under the shadow of the Almighty. He does not just occasionally visit this secret place, but instead, he makes it a habitual dwelling place. He refreshes his spirit with fasting and prayer. He is not critical of his brother or sister, he does not entertain gossip, neither is he judgmental. He is not covetous, nor neglectful. He is not filled with anger, bitterness, and resentment.

He does not harbour animosity and hatred in his heart. He does not lie, he does not steal, he does not commit adultery, and he is not a fornicator. In essence, he gives no room to the devil in his life. His life is filled with the glory of God because he has made the Lord his refuge. He is not looking to the wicked one for help. He is looking to the hills from whence cometh his help , as is David s encouragement in Psalm 121.

When one is free of all the elements of sin, then without a question of doubt, he is wearing the whole armour of Jesus Christ. In the armour lies the word of God, the blood of Jesus and the name of Jesus. These are the weapons of our warfare, and they are not carnal but they are mighty through God to the pulling down of strongholds.

Remember you will not be able to use these weapons until you are spiritually dressed, and robed in righteousness, just as Paul encourages us to do in the book of Ephesians.

STEP TWO: USING THE ARMOUR AND THE WEAPONS

For the weapons of our warfare are not carnal, but mighty through God to the pulling down of strongholds. Casting down imaginations and every high thing that exalteth itself against the knowledge of God and bringing into captivity every thought to the obedience of Christ. 2 CORINTHIANS 10-4

THE NAME OF JESUS

As mentioned in Step One, our armour consists of the word of God, the name of Jesus, the power of the Holy Ghost and the blood of Jesus. If we examine the behaviour of the members of the deliverance group that came to me we can establish that not only were they wearing the armour of Jesus Christ, but they also had weapons at their disposal.

These weapons were mighty enough, through God, to pull down the many strongholds that I needed to be delivered from. These members took the authority that the Lord had invested in them and used those weapons. One of these is very powerful indeed. This is simply, the name of Jesus.

These members knew that there is power in that name and they used it boldly and fearlessly against those demons. I am emphasising the word authority here as derived from the Greek word **exousia**, meaning the right to exercise power of authority , or, the liberty, ability or strength which one is endued with, to exercise that power .

In effect their power lay in the fact that they had prepared themselves to do the job. They had equipped and renewed minds, and the enemy was keeping no secrets for them. They were therefore able to use that name with complete authority.

In the book of Acts, the Apostles were healing many people and casting out devils in the name of Jesus. When the leaders realised that there was so much power and authority in the name, they became fearful that they would lose their glory. Some of them could have been exorcists and false preachers.

They realised that the power to perform those miracles lay in the use of the name of Jesus. In their paranoia, the bible tells us the following:

And when they had called the apostles and had beaten them, they commanded them that they should not speak in the name of Jesus and let them go . ACTS 5: 40

It is evident therefore that the politicians of the day were afraid of the name. Scholars and teachers were afraid of the name and heads of government were afraid of the name. If theological scoffers were afraid, philosophers of the day were afraid, how much more were demons? The bible tells us that:

At the name of Jesus, every knee should bow of things in heaven, and things under the earth. And that every tongue should confess that Jesus Christ is the Lord to the Glory of God the father. PHILIPPIANS. 2:11-1

Another important point to note, however, is that although there is power in the name of Jesus, there are devils that call upon that name as well. Witchcraft workers are using the name and iniquity workers are using the name. I used to use the name when I was in the occultic world. However, the use of the name was ineffective because I had no authority to use it. When I called upon the name of Jesus, it was just like calling Mary or Tom.

Note that even when I was coming out of that world through illness and was calling on that name it was still futile. Why? Simply because I was still using it without authority. I had no solid relationship with the Lord, my mind was unrenewed, I was not living a righteous life, I was not baptised, I was not filled with the Holy Spirit, and in essence, I was not a blood washed child of God. Accordingly, the name was like feather in my mouth. As you progress through these chapters you will learn how this name has now become dynamite for me because I now have the authority to use it. Hallelujah! What a privilege!

THE BLOOD OF JESUS

Having called on the name of Jesus and commanded those demons to leave, the deliverance team repeatedly called on the Blood of Jesus . I have now found that when this piece of weaponry is used in conjunction with the armour of God, it is such a powerful piece of ammunition that even the devil in hell has to quickly vacate the scene.

I am positive that wherever the blood of Jesus is used that it leaves behind invisible trails of spiritual blood that we cannot see with the naked eye. However, demons are very sensitive to these trails and whenever they see it they have to vacate the scene. I believe that there is spiritual fire in the blood and that if they dare to step on that trace of blood that they would merely melt into nothingness.

Earlier in this book I discussed a powerful deliverance service in my home during which I had delivered a young man who had been demonised since birth. When the demons returned in the dead of the night to carry out their assignments and switched off all the lights, they looked at my house and saw that it was covered with the blood of Jesus.

They could not venture near my home and they swiftly told their master, We can t go there, that place is covered by the blood of Jesus. I can just picture their trembling spooky faces as they fled from the scene.

The blood reminds Satan of an incident that he just cannot stand the thought of. It reminds him of the crucifixion and the redemptive work of Jesus Christ. It reminds him of the humiliation that he suffered in the presence of his demons when Jesus descended to his domain and snatched the keys of hell from him.

It reminds him of his final judgement. It reminds him that he is on borrowed time. It tells him that he has no future, for no one that will be bound for a thousand years has any future. He knows that after this time his lease will be up and that he will then be finished with.

Satan is liar and a murderer who is spending the longest recorded time in history on death row. He knows that judgement has been already passed. He knows that he is only waiting for that day to come. However, unlike many others on the death row, who have a peaceful death, it will not be so for the wicked one. He has done so much wrong to the human race that he has to suffer before the final judgement. Consequently, the blood reminds him of all of these things. He therefore has no other choice, but to run trembling with fear at the mention of the blood.

When I was attacked by the devil, my little boy also came under constant and severe satanic oppression. One night when he was about the age of six, he went to bed and evil spirits came to visit him.

After this time this poor child's life became a constant nightmare. Demons would invariably visit him in his sleep, and of course, his young little mind could not comprehend what was going on. All that he could do was to give me detailed explanations of the nasty monsters that were appearing in his sleep.

One morning he woke up to tell me of a visitation which he had from a purported monster. He told me that it came, placed a lock around his neck and said to him "A holy, B holy and C holy" and that after the monster had said this he was unable to speak. This demonstrates that these demons are intelligent beings that understand the reasoning ability of a six-year-old child. As such they used child like thought processes to play their nasty tricks on him.

When the child told me, I was taken aback with rage. In fact I was practically maniacal. I remember thinking to myself, "Lord, what wickedness." It was then that the Lord told me what to do. I quickly advised my son that whenever he saw those things in his sleep he should keep repeating to himself "The Blood of Jesus".

"But, mummy I wont remember that!" he had said, but I assured him that he would remember, and that all that he needed to do was to practice it.

Then one night they came back. My son told me that the moment that he saw them he began to call on the blood of Jesus. He said that the demons turned around, looked at him, and said. "The blood of what?" And they began to run! Hallelujah to God, even a young innocent child can learn how to use the blood of Jesus against evils.

Demons are wicked things and they have no respect for age. Whenever your small children tell you that they saw a monster in their sleep begin to pray for them. They have seen a demon. Moreover, if you do not take authority over that force your child can be severely affected through out his/ her life.

There is also another lesson in this. The bible tells us that when the disciples tried to rebuke the little children in the book of Matthew, Jesus said:

Suffer little children and forbid then not to come unto me: For of such is the kingdom of heaven. St Matthew 19:14

In order to possess the righteousness that will allow you to take authority and to use the armour of Jesus Christ, you must have the faith of a young child. The faith that young children have in their parents, and that which they would have in God.

We should be as innocent as a little child. My child knew that if mummy said that it would work then it had to and he was an innocent child. His authority lay in his faith and his childlike righteousness. He unquestioningly took the authority, used that mighty weapon and it worked. As long as you have that type of faith and that righteousness, then take the authority in the name of Jesus.

THE WORD OF GOD

If ye abide in me, and my words abide in you, ye shall ask what ye will and it shall be done unto you. St John 15:7

I knew nothing about the importance of the word of God let alone how to use it out of Christ. Nevertheless, once I began to seek the Lord and to read the Bible, His words rapidly became alive to me.

When I read initially that I could only be delivered through prayer and fasting, I believed it. Then I read that the effectual fervent prayer of a righteous man availeth much , and I also accepted that.

I then placed those realities within my mind and began to meditate upon them. I realised that I had some stubborn demons residing in me, which would not leave just merely by praying but through prayer accompanied by fasting.

I also realised that I was not a righteous person and that it would take a righteous person to command those demons to leave. With the truth of those rhema words within me, I immediately changed the way that I was praying and began to pray that the Lord would send me a righteous person. In addition, I prayed that that person would be on prayer and fasting. I believed in God s words that were there in the bible.

God is not a man that he should lie. As such the Lord sent me righteous people who were praying to deliver me and I was delivered.

As a deliverance minister, I know that I have the word of God dwelling within me, and I use it with faith against the enemies. I remind them of certain chapters in the bible such as:

The Lord has given me power and authority over all devils and to cure diseases . St. Luke 9:1-2

I further remind them that in the book of Matthew:

The Lord has given to me the keys of the kingdom of heaven and that what I bind on earth is already bound in heaven and what I loose on earth is already loose in heaven. St Matthew 16:19

I am also aware from my own experience that in most cases of the demonised there is always a strongman, who is the head demon and who will control the lesser ones. I know that once he leaves the scene then the others will obediently follow. I will therefore make reference to the book of Matthew 12 and verse 29, which tells me that:

In order to enter a strong man s house, then we first would have to bind the strong man and then we can spoil his goods. Matthew 12:29

Take his goods means to remove the demons that are under his control. I will therefore take authority over that strong man and that will make the whole deliverance process much easier for me.

The word of God is a very powerful weapon to use against the enemy. Even Satan himself tried to use the written word against Jesus. In the book of Matthew chapter 4, Satan came to Jesus to tempt Him. In rebuking the devil, Jesus used no weapons other than the word of God.

When Satan tried to tempt Him, Jesus quoted scriptures from Deuteronomy while the devil tried to trick Him with the word by misquoting the Psalms.

After being defeated the devil fled from the presence of the Lord. The devil, therefore, is well aware of the importance of the written word.

Demons will swear at you and tell you that you are a liar. They will tell you all sorts of nasty things when you are attempting to expel them. Nevertheless, they dare not tell you that the word of God is not true, for even evil spirits know that God is not a man that He should lie. When we have our armour on and in its rightful place, and we use the word of God with authority as a weapon of our warfare, the devil has no choice but to vacate the scene.

Chapter 12

Knowing Your Calling

Then He called His disciples together and gave them power and authority over all devils and to cure diseases and He sent them to preach the kingdom of God and to heal the sick' Luke 9: 1-2

DIVINE PURPOSE

I believe that in these last days, we as children of God will need to come together and storm the gates of hell so that the Lord can pour out His spirit as in former days. In so doing, man will come to the realisation that God has not gone to sleep. After all, the devil is busy recruiting his end time forces, so why shouldn t our God also draft in His end time warriors?

Mere evangelism will not work for the church in these last days. People need to see the hands of God working in their lives. In their time of trial they need to run to a healing ministry and, like the woman at the well, return to their friends telling them Come see a man .

They need to see diseases being healed; they need to see the churches picking up the pieces when the hospitals can find no remedy. They need to see demons being cast out of the lives of God s children.

They need a sign from heaven. It is this need that has drawn souls to End Time Healing Ministry and which is still drawing them. As Christians we have become too complacent, settling for second best. God has called us to be saved, and as such we think we have somehow reached and that our purpose for being is fulfilled. This is a dangerous misconception, for there is significantly deeper depth and higher heights in God, which so many Christians are not taping into.
Speaking to King Solomon in the book of Chronicles, the Lord says:

If my people, which are called by my name, shall humble themselves, and pray, and seek my face, and turn from their wicked ways. Then will I hear from heaven and will forgive their sins and will heal their land.
2 CHRONICLES 7:14

God spoke these words concerning the Israelites in ancient days, and those words are still being echoed on our streets, in our homes, on the buses, in the trains and in our churches, and from the pulpit to the pew. God cannot heal the land through Pastors who have taken the glory off the throne and are wearing it around their necks.

He cannot heal our land through church members who are so lost in their self-righteousness that they forget that salvation is not about self-centredness. He will not heal His nation through religious empire builders. He wants us to humble ourselves and to seek His face. God does not want us to draw the glory to ourselves, or into our bank accounts. That is using God and no sin will go unpunished.

This is why we are told that on the day of judgement, there will be signs and wonders and that the last shall be the first and the first shall be last. God s desire is for us to be yielded earthen vessels, into which he can pour his spirit.

We need to humble ourselves and ask the Lord to re-ignite our ministries. We want some upper room outpouring in our midst. We want unlearned men to be so filled with the knowledge of God that the religious Pharisees will again ask the question,

Isn t that the unlearned one?

We want God to move the veil of brass from over the heavens so that our prayers can penetrate through open windows to the throne room of God in heaven. Only then will we begin to experience the glory of God. We want to feel and experience some end time Pentecostal rain, pouring into our ministries and into our lives.

However, we sometimes seem to be so caught up with our religion, that we tend to forget our true purpose as children of God. We need to disregard the focus on religion and to take on the glory of God, and strive to see the true purpose of God for our lives. We need a touch of Glory.

I remember one morning after I had completed a wonderful devotion with the Lord and his wonderful angels. I had to go on an errand so I took the bus. As I was sitting in a quiet corner on the upper deck, a thought came to me. I wondered whether it was really possible for us to see the Lord.
I immediately asked Him.

Lord, can we see you?

No my child, He replied, but you can see my Glory.

Then show me your glory, I said.

Sitting there on that upper deck, right in the middle of the traffic, on a bright summer s day and amidst the hustle and bustle and activity all around me, I experienced the Glory of God.

The Lord said to me:

My child look yonder.

When I looked into the sky, I saw an indenture of a huge face, and from the area of the face, I saw beautiful streaks of golden rays dashing across the earth. They were so beautiful that I was unable to fix my eyes on them for a long period. It was sheer glory, and it was so magnificent that I cannot describe the scene.

Those beautiful rays were dashing over the corners of the earth. However, when I looked around to see whether the rays were being sent to the four corners of the earth, I suddenly realised that some places were not getting the glory of God. There were some areas to which the rays did not extend.

Then I heard the Lord telling me that there are regions in which He is unable to shine His glory and that this is because of the sinful nature of those people who inhabit those domains. Certain places have become so polluted with sin that God cannot even bear to look there.

The blood of innocent people is crying from many soils. Man has turned from worshipping God and is worshipping idols. Animals are given precedence over God. Dirty stagnant water is being worshipped. For some, Buddha sits quite composed on his pedestals, while Allah is worshipped instead of God and Mohammed and even Haile-Selassi live on.

How could the Glory of God be shone in those places? God will not take second place and He will certainly not share His Glory with no man let alone the devil. We look for the Glory of God in Israel, but it is not there. We search Pakistan and India and it is gone. It is gone from Afghanistan, from the Middle East, and the Far East.

In fact I am very weary about these areas, and as I have told my congregation, I feel that this is where the battle of the Armageddon will be fought. When I had just come to the Lord I became a member of Bible way Church. During that time I had a vision that has greatly troubled me and will always live with me. In this

vision, a great bear walked into the church and he began to roll around and growl and then he began to speak as though in great pain.
He said that the war will be fought and it will begin in Afghanistan.

I am very weary of those places and we, as God s people must keep our eyes on that area of the world. Any people that do not serve the Lord will only succeed in opening doors for the devil to come into their territory and to influence them into all manner of evil.

I also realised from my visions that the presence of the Lord can be over an entire nation or country, but that His glory may be unable to penetrate certain areas of that place.

This is due to the territorial spirits that are ruling those regions and the strongmen that are in charge there. For example, God s glory cannot penetrate the West End of London, England, because of the strongmen of prostitution and drug abuse that are ruling there.

His glory will not penetrate Soho because of the ruling territorial spirits of homosexuality and lesbianism, and neither can Bermondsey be fully penetrated because of the territorial spirits of terror, prejudice and occultism.

I live in the heart of the city, very close to Tower Bridge. During the daytime, this place is thriving with tourists who arrive from all over the world and all walks of life to see the many local attractions. However, when night falls, the city is a different scenario. The place becomes extremely dark, dreadful and frightening. When I prayed about the neighbourhood the Lord showed me that several nasty strongmen and several vicious territorial spirits rule the entire area.

He showed me that the blood of those beheaded in the London dungeon still cry from the streets, and that the strong man is still at work above the city. He showed me that the territorial spirits of witchcraft are still around and that they take over the city by night.

He also showed me that strong men of blood and war are dwelling around the area of the war museum, while other spirits of racism, pride, hatred, and bitterness are still at work there.

On learning of this information, my team and I went into fasting and all night prayer, and under the instruction of the Holy Spirit and the guidance of the Lord, we went into four directions and anointed the streets and the buildings. We pulled down territorial spirits and broke strongholds. Nevertheless, we are very aware that there is still a lot to be done in this area.

Just recently I also questioned the Lord about the bloodshed in Kingston Jamaica. I tried to understand why bloodshed was so rampant in a nation that is so religious. The Lord showed me that the cities of Kingston and Spanish Town also have some very nasty territorial spirits of bloodshed, which date back to the activities of the buccaneers in Jamaica. In addition, strongmen of witchcraft, brutality and slavery were transported from Africa.

Further to this, the Lord gave me the vision of how these territorial spirits and strongholds need to be broken from over the nation before His glory can fully penetrate the entire country.

Jamaica is not short of the word of God; however, if we do not take authority over these nasty territorial spirits and strongmen, and begin to rip down their walls and fortifications, there will continue to be bloodshed in its city.

If only we could all see the glory of God! If only we could all be completely lost in it! If only man could understand the purity and awesomeness of Gods Glory! Then would we be in a position to realise the astounding beauty of heaven and the overwhelming omnipotence of God. Churches need to wake up and break down the walls and partitions and begin to do real business for the king.

Only recently, I was again transported to heaven. On this occasion I walked on streets of purest material, and as I was entering a particular area, I heard a melodious singing, from a most beautiful choir of voices. I moved towards this choir and when I got there, I found a huge convention was in progress and many churches were presented. I saw flags of all nations.

I went into one of the churches and the choir was singing a most beautiful song. They sang superbly and after listening to them for a while I went into another church. Here I found that they were singing the same song to the same tune as the former church. I moved from church to church and continued to find the members all singing the same song to the same tune. I woke up and realised that God had revealed to me that there is no religion in heaven.

It became clear to me that we need to stop the religious squabbles and get on with business for the kingdom. We want to be real kingdom builders. We need to begin preparing for the return of the Lord.

Contrary to some of our beliefs that we will be living in heaven forever with Jesus, this very earth is where He will be coming back to set up His Kingdom. Therefore, we need to really begin to prepare the earth for His return.

God wants to pour out his spirit upon all flesh and He wants to begin with you. If you have a ministry, then God wants His gifts to be manifested in you so that souls can be born for His kingdom. The Lord wants to return to find a people who are aware of the awesome power of God that is invested in them, and are using the gifts of the spirits for the establishment of His Kingdom here on earth.

This is a time that my church is preparing for and we are drawing in and delivering souls for the kingdom of God.

In the next few chapters I will share with you precisely how we are functioning as an End Time Healing Ministry, and why souls are being attracted to this church.

Chapter 13

Loose Him & Let Him Go

The spirit of the Lord is upon me. Because the Lord hath anointed me to preach good tidings unto the meek. He hath send me to bind up the broken hearted, to proclaim liberty to the captives and the opening of prison to them that are bound. To proclaim the acceptable year of the Lord, and the day of vengeance of our God. To comfort all that mourn. Isaiah 61:1-2

DEMONIC ENCOUNTERS

It was only a few weeks after the ministry had started that I had my first encounter with the demonised. At that time, services were still being held at my home. A young man came to join our fellowship that at first seemed rather enthusiastic. About the time of his second visit, in the midst of a very powerful service, he fell to the ground and began to sweat, kick and fight.

He continued with this manifestation, frothing at the mouth and roaring like a lion. He rapidly became completely out of control, while we continued to rebuke the demons and ask them to leave in the name of Jesus. At that time I was pregnant and Satan made sure that he fell on me so that I lost the baby.

I would like to pause here to give a word of advice to pregnant mothers. These women should, as far as possible, avoid getting involved with deliverance services. At those times they become very vulnerable and weak and they may find that both they and their child/ren are exposed to the kingdom of darkness.

We continued working with this young man but as we proceeded, the situation became more frightening. He began to choke and his oxygen supply appeared as though it was cutting off. His face also began to change colour. You could see that he was choking. To say that I was petrified would be an understatement. I called for an ambulance.

By the time the paramedics arrived, he was in such a state that it took many of the male staff to pin him to the ground. He was railing, kicking, and behaving like a completely mad person.

They gave him oxygen and called for backup staff. His condition was so bad that they all handled him with gloves. As far as they were concerned, someone must have given him a thorough beating in his head and they were not going to do anything that would hide the evidence.

After stabilising him, he was rushed off to hospital while the police stayed behind to question us. They wanted to know if there was a fight and if he had received any injuries to his head. A few minutes after they left, my husband rang back to say that the young man was well and that he wanted to speak with me.

When I questioned him, he could not remember anything that had happened to him. He asked why he was in the hospital and wanted me to explain to him what had happened. I later realised that this is exactly how a person who is demonised would behave.

This was not the young man's doing. His behaviour in fact, was completely due to the demons that were inside him. During his fit he had displayed the strength of about thirty men. I also realised later that this strength was not his own, but rather that of the many unclean spirits that were dwelling in him.

I was so embarrassed after he had gone to the hospital and after all the commotion that this had caused in my home. I felt completely useless and ineffective. I knew that I was a born again child of God, I was filled with the Holy Ghost and was called for service. However, I was totally unprepared for this type of demonic encounter, and the scene that it created at my house. Due to this incident, I lost many young, immature and inexperienced saints.

Immediately after this occurrence, I went away for a break, during which time I questioned the Lord about the incident. I received a word of knowledge that confirmed that I had not made any preparation for the deliverance and that there were things that needed to be dealt with in the life of the young man before he could be delivered.

While I was away, this man went to many places looking for help. By then his attacks were getting more severe and he was desperate to return to living a normal life. Upon my return, I was informed that he had become like a roaring lion in one of these deliverance services that he had been to and that they had tried desperately to deliver him, but could not.

During our first meeting after my return from abroad, the Lord placed it upon my heart to speak about ungodly ties. I was dealing with this topic and was placing emphasis on the cult which is called "The Brotherhood" when he began to pour out his heart.

He told us that he was a member of this secret cult and began to give us small details about his initiation.

Suddenly he sat back in his chair and began to take authority for himself, against that secret sect. He denounced his involvement with them and spoke of an inner circle meeting that he should have attended. He asked that his name be removed from that list. Then he began to speak of a water spirit, which he knew was inside him. As soon as he made mention of that mermaid demon, however, he became dumb.

By now I was feeling stronger in the Lord, and was adamant that those nasty demons were not going to overpower us again. I took control of the situation and began to pray. The young man then began to speak but was visibly in much pain. I was determined that those evils were leaving there and then and I took authority over them and cast them out in the name of our Lord Jesus. Yes they railed and they ranted, and they tried to get us to call the ambulance but they had to leave. It was wonderful to see the peace and complete calm that came over the young man after he was delivered.

A FAILED DELIVERANCE

Evidently we had failed at setting that man free during the first attempt at deliverance and there are obvious reasons for this.

b) PREPARATION FOR THE DELIVERANCE TEAM

A deliverance team must be prepared for a deliverance service otherwise there may be casualties. Demons are very vicious and powerful things and we must be equipped with the almighty power that surpasses their power so that we are able to successfully overcome them.

We must prepare ourselves through getting the rhema word, that is, the inspired word, and the logos word, i.e. the written word, of God inside of us. We need to strengthen our beings through prayer and fasting to stay in the presence of the Lord. We must cleanse our hearts and make sure that we are anointed with the healing and deliverance power of God.

b) PREPARATION FOR THE PERSON WHO IS TO BE DELIVERED

The deliverance should begin with a counselling session where we establish whether they are prepared to let go of those demons or not. If a possessed person is quite happy to keep his evils with him, then it is very difficult for you to take those from him. If I have squatters in my property, and I want them to leave, then I have to ask them to go. Moreover squatters do not leave quite easily, and you often have to either enforce the law, or vigorously throw them out by force.

Initially this young man had not been prepared to evict his squatters so they were quite happy to stay with him. However when it comes to deliverance, there must be a desire to evict the enemy and be loosed from his grip.

Many people go to occultists asking them for power, and what they receive from these witches are powerful evils, which take over their bodies and their lives. With the same earnest that they had asked for this power from the enemy, so should they ask that they be relinquished of these forces.

c) COUNSELLING THE VICTIM TO RECOGNISE THE DANGER

Many individuals just do not see any thing wrong with being involved in the realm of darkness. In fact, spiritual darkness has been introduced to some as spirit of Light. The devil quoted the scriptures to the Lord, so he knows the bible very well. In fact many witches use certain scriptures to do their incantations.

Some people think that because a so-called spiritualist uses the bible and provides chapters to read with the burning of candles, that that means that they are not doing witchcraft. We must remember that the bible says that Satan himself is transformed into an angel of light to deceive us. (2Corinthians 11: 14]

This is one of Satan s biggest tactics, which he has used for centuries and that he is still using to deceive us. I was so caught up in this trap that I used to daily light a candle to pray believing that I was doing a good thing.

We should also realise that most of these candles have been chanted over by witches, and in addition, they have used occultic oils and other tools to load these candles with evil.

This can be nothing other than evil and is certainly a snare and trap of the enemy. Many people are being deceived in this manner and it often takes a great deal of encouragement to get them to see the evil that they have been involved in.

One of my most recent victims is a young woman who for the purpose of example I will call Maria . She came from America to study in London and as she was eagerly seeking the Lord, she enrolled on a course at one of London s Universities to do some courses in spiritualism. One of our members with whom she was living found out that she was really seeking the Lord and led her to the church. As soon as I saw her, I received a word of knowledge that she was quite confused and needed counselling.

I made the appointment with her and asked that she bring her course prospectus to me. I was not surprised when I saw the course titles. Amongst others were meditation, yoga and transcendental projection, magical geometry, candle burning, tarot reading, self-actualisation, positive thinking and other magical arts. This young naive girl who had desired to seek God was now studying to become a witch with other students in one of Britain s top universities.

If we take for example the topic of meditation, we understand that this is a practice where the student is told to blank your mind completely in an effort to gain peace .

Once you have become an expert at this, you then begin to learn how to float out of your body and to project yourself into other places. This is a commonly used practice for witches who do this to cause evil and destruction. Armed with this knowledge it is easy to understand then why people have been found strangled in their sleep with no apparent explanation.

This can be as a result of an evil witch leaving their body behind and projecting into the victim s room while they have been asleep and then destroying them. In most cases, they are under assignment from the kingdom of darkness. This is a very real activity and it really does happen. The bible clearly tells us in the book of 2 Thessalonians chapter 5, that man is tripartite, being spirit, soul and body.

Paul also speaks of a man that he saw when he went to heaven and did not know whether he was in the body or the spirit. When John was on the Isle of Patmos, the Lord took him out of his body and into the spirit to give him the Revelations. Without question, witches can leave their bodies in what is known as astral projection, however, this is such a dangerous act that I would like to draw particular attention to it, so as to warn people to stay clear of it.

In addition to the evil for which astral projection can be used, there is also another danger of which manner participants are unaware. When your spirit leaves your body, a space is left where the spirit should be. It is common to find that when witches leave their bodies, they return to find that there are other occupants now inhabiting that space and that now they are actually sharing the body with others.

I realised through discussion with the young man that was involved in the brotherhood, that he was frequently involved in meditation and could have left his body on several occasions. When he came for deliverance, he had the strength of an elephant and the weight of a rhinoceros. We were dealing with a body, which was packed with legions of darkness.

Many people have left their bodies to carry out their evils and have not been able to return. As a result they have been found dead in their sleep. No evil can stand against a blood washed child of God. Moreover, when you are constantly dwelling in the secret place of the most high then you are protected under the shadow of the wings of the Almighty.

This means that an innumerable company of angels are protecting you with drawn swords. In addition, their job is to smite the enemy; as such when an enemy leaves his or her body to destroy a child of God, the angel of God can smite him. He is treading on dangerous ground and as such this is a very risky practice.

Equally dangerous is tarot card reading. Each of these cards has a picture on it, which represents a Greek god or goddess, who is responsible for some increase or destruction in life. In fact, these are idols that were at one time being worshipped and as such there is a demon associated with every card. I distinctly remember the many tormented nights that I had experienced after using the tarot. On occasions it was as if the very evil on the cards would come to visit me at nights.

Reading the cards themselves was an experience. As the reader you would examine the card and suddenly you would be telling people things about themselves from the picture on the card that you know nothing about and they would be nodding their heads in agreement with you. It was as though the demons on the cards took over your voice. In addition, after the session you would feel very drained. It was as if all of your life substance had been drained from you. The tarot is very dangerous and something that no one should even look at. As soon as you look at them you begin to feel the heavy oppression around you.

Everything on Maria s course was very dangerous to study. Magical mathematics, is also known as numerology, and is the science of using numbers to read into one s life and to play games of chance. It is a form of clairvoyance and like the other techniques , should be left alone.

I was not surprised that when I looked at the young woman, I received a word of knowledge that she had the spirit of a witch dwelling within her. I took time to sit with her and point out the dangers of her witchcraft course. I got her to sever all ungodly ties and then presented the Gospel of Jesus Christ to her, which she accepted. She has now been delivered and is happily walking with the Lord.

In the case of the young man, with the many demons in him, once he had made his confessions and publicly denounced the enemy from his life his deliverance became an easy one. Not only did he now accept that what he was involved in was wrong, but he also saw the danger in it and was more than anxious to get those squatters out.

Demons are squatters that have no right to possess the body of humans. They rightfully belong to the abyss, and they should be cast out of the body and should be told to go wherever the Lord sends them.

Do not ever worry about what happens to them when they leave. Many people have asked me what happens to them, and whether there is a danger of them going into someone else.

Demons should be told to go where the Lord sends them and not into the pit of hell. The Lord knows exactly where to send them - remember that he did send some into pigs and I have seen dogs swim but I have never seen a pig swimming.

Jesus knew that those pigs could not swim so he sent those legions right into the bottom of the ocean. Let the Lord have His way. You do what you have to do and ask the Lord to do that which you cannot.

There is a two-fold preparation for deliverance. As the person conducting the deliverance you should be covered by the blood and should ask the Lord for guidance, and wisdom, and the person to be delivered should be counselled.

During the counselling session we should find out what kind of demons we are dealing with, and also what strongholds will need to be broken from his/her life. We will learn about the doorways that have been opened to allow those demons in and we should be able to assist the person in breaking the strongholds, kicking the demons out and closing those doors.

d) MANAGING THE PROCESS AFTER DELIVERANCE

When the unclean spirit is gone out of a man, he walketh through dry places, seeking rest and findeth none. Then he said I would return into my house from whence I came out. And when he is come he findeth it empty, swept and garnished.

Then goeth he and taketh with himself, seven other spirits more wicked than himself, and they enter in and dwell there. And the last state of the man is worst than the first. St Matthew 12:43-45

Now after the young man who is under discussion in this chapter was delivered, we did not know that he should be counselled. This is not something that I had received when I had been delivered.

In my case, there was a lesser need as I was fully persuaded that God would now see me through. Moreover, I had really accepted the Lord, so I truly wanted him in my heart. However, in the case of many people who come for deliverance, all that they want is to be free from the oppression and then to go back into sin. God just does not work like that.

Sometimes the demonised refuse to give up their sinful way of life and without counselling they will return to their former ways after deliverance. This can be very dangerous, and in fact, experience has taught me that it is better to let a demonised person stay with the demons rather than casting them out and then allowing that person to remain in sin.

The scripture above explains what happens to the demons after they leave a person. Once this entity has been cast out it will go roaming seeking a lodging place. The bible did not say if it does not find any, but rather and findeth none meaning that it will find no other abode.

Its next plan of action is to return to its former owner to see whether the Lord has taken up residence in the life of that person. If He has not and the demons should find the space still available, then he will go and get seven worst demons than himself and they will come back. This time it would have been better if the person had not been delivered because the last state of this person would be worst than the previous.

Even before introducing deliverance to a person he should be told about God s plan of salvation and should be offered repentance. This scripture should also be read along with others on repentance, baptism, and the infilling of the Holy Spirit. The Bible tells us that with the mouth confession is made unto sin therefore sin should be confessed and the Lord should be accepted. Then the deliverance can begin.

I find that unless this is done then the deliverance process will become a very tiresome and weary job. Don t forget that Satan knows when you are not getting it right, and his job is to allow his evils to wear you out. Moreover, you should ensure that you have your back up team.

Deliverance is like running the medley relay. As soon as the athletes have run a leg and begin to get weary, it s time to change the baton. You should not allow yourself to get too weary in a deliverance service. As soon as you begin to get tired then change partners, or pass the bat on.

Shortly after the young man was delivered he left the church and he became quite nasty and aggressive. I tried to encourage him to come back to church but he did not want to know. One Sunday, he walked into service and he was so restless that he could not sit with the congregation. He drew a chair and sat in the far back of the church. I had a word of knowledge that the enemy had sent him on assignment to break up the church.

As soon as the anointing fell, he began to manifest demons. I did not try to deliver him. The deliverance team saw what I did and they did exactly the same thing. I was prepared to deliver him but not in the middle of my service. He was not going to allow one other thirsty soul to leave the church. I had learnt from my mistakes.

Yes some demons will flee once the anointing falls in a service and if possessed individuals are in a sermon that is charged with the presence of the Holy Spirit then deliverance will automatically take place.

However, if a person has been sent on an assignment to destroy the work of the Lord, then we have to use wisdom in such circumstances. I was adamant that if he needed deliverance then he should see me for counselling.

He stayed there with his manifestation while we offered deliverance to those who were genuinely in need. Afterwards, he got up and went away cursing. That was certainly a plan of the enemy.

After his previous deliverance, he had continued coming for a while after which he went straight back to the kingdom of darkness. This time he was so tightly held by them that he became their agent. He had not fully accepted the Lord and consequently became a victim as described in St Matthew 12.

The experience, which I had with this demonised person, became a solid foundation, on which I have built my deliverance ministry. Unfortunately, there are many deliverance ministries springing up, in which the demons are the real heroes.

I have seen evils running loose while so called deliverance ministers yell words like:

Get out! Manifest and get out! Manifest and get out! Tell us your name! Who sent you!

The evil spirits will have the individuals running all around the building and would be telling all sorts of lies.

Satan is the father of lies so why would we want to listen to him? Furthermore we are actually sinning by listening to demons. Those are unclean and familiar spirits speaking to us and we must never listen to them. Once I heard a demon telling a deliverance minister in a rather humiliating, nasty and coarse voice:

Oh you are a strong man! I could do a lot with your spirit. If I could get your spirit then I will think of releasing that of the young woman, there are lots of things that I could do with your spirit!

The whole church found those words so funny. They were observing an unclean spirit, and were being entertained by it. Looking back, it was such a sickening sight. Those demons should not have been allowed to speak, they should have been cast out. They danced around in the woman until this strong minister was so wearied that he had to give up. Those spirits had won.

If we do not know how to deal with devils then we should leave them alone and to someone who does know how to deal with them. We do not all have the same gifts and most certainly are not all trained in the same area of the gospel. Neither are we all called to the same ministry.

This can be a very dangerous ministry and unless one is called for this area of work, it should be left alone. Remember that not even the disciples of Jesus could loose the possessed boy of Matthew 17.

Although it is a fulfilling and much needed ministry, to the untrained and unprepared there can be casualties. I have been a victim and have lost many babies on the battlefield. However the gates of hell will not prevail against me, and I will do that which the Lord has called me to do. In addition, I will do it with all my heart, my soul and my mind and I will continue to give the glory to God.

Chapter 14

Strongholds

> For the weapons of our warefare are not carnal but mighty through God, to the putting down of strongholds. Casting down imagination and every high thing that exaleth itself against the knowledge of God, and bring into captivity every thought to the obedience of Christ.
> 2 Corinthians 10: 4-5

DEMONS VS STRONGHOLDS: THE DIFFERENCES

As the Lord continued to manifest His healing, saving and deliverance power in the ministry, souls were now being attracted from all walks of life and with many needs. Many were demonised and were delivered, but many had such strongholds and bondage in their lives that one had to carefully discern between both.

A person can have a very bad habit, which stems from a stronghold in his/her life and we can easily assume that this is a demonic oppression when in fact it is not. He/she might merely be in need of inner healing. It might just a cry for help.

It is possible for a strong man, that is, a demon, to have a stronghold in your life, and certainly every stronghold is as a result of the work of the enemy in your life, however, a stronghold is not a demon.

WHAT IS A STRONGHOLD?

According to Vine 1098 the term stronghold comes from the Greek **ochuroma**, which means a fortress or to make firm . A fortress is a very high, strong and defenced place, similar to a prison. Many of us have been to visit someone in prison and have seen the high powerful and iron structures that are built to keep the prisoners in.

Paul, speaking about strongholds in the book of 2 Corinthians 10:4, likens these strongholds to such fortresses.

Strongholds are fortifications that the enemy has built in your soulish realm, in the realm of the spirit and also in the flesh.

We know that man is soul, body and spirit. The body is like a car, which carries an engine. The engine can be compared with the spirit; the car would not be able to move without it. Within the engine are others parts that are also very important to the car and upon which it relies for movement. These parts when combined can be likened to the soul.

Your body relates to the natural and earthly things around you, through your senses, and the bible further describes your body as the temple of the spirit (1Cor. 3: 16), and as the only part that dies at physical death (Jas.2: 26).

THE SPIRIT

The Hebrew word for spirit is **Ruach**, while the New Testament Greek word is **Pneuma**. Both refer to an invisible force . The spirit of man therefore is the intellect, will, mind, conscience and other invisible faculties that make man a free moral being and a rational thinker.

Both the spirit and the soul are immortal. They are very closely related, and it is sometimes difficult to distinguish between them.

It is with the spirit that you reach God and communicate with Him. You worship in the spirit, pray in the spirit and sing in the spirit. When the body dies, it is the spirit that lives on. Therefore the spirit is your highest being, and this is why we are commanded to keep the body holy, as it is the vessel for the spirit man.

The spirit of man was fully operative before the fall, during the time when man was in close communion with God. At that time his spirit man was fully functional and his flesh was subdued. However, when sin came, man suffered a spiritual death, which suppressed his spirit thus separating him from God, as consequence, man s constant quest is to be re-connected to the Almighty.

Some people say that we need to get connected with God, when in truth we need to be re-connected .

THE SOUL

The Hebrew word for soul is **Nephesh**, which means a living being, the invisible part of man. The Greek word is **Psuche**, which denotes the breath of life and the soul in its various meanings. For example: It is the natural life of the body. It is the seat of the sentient element in man that by which he perceives, reflects, feels and desires. It is the seat of will and purpose, and of the appetite.

Generally speaking, the soul feels and the spirit knows .

According to Vines:

The spirit may be recognised as the life principle bestowed on man by God, the soul as the resulting life constituted in the individual, the body being the material organism animated by soul and spirit. [VINES 1997: 1067].

WHERE ARE THESE STRONGHOLDS BUILT?

The bible tells us that man is tripartite. That he is body soul and spirit. In the book of Thessalonians, Paul in closing says:

And the very God of peace, sanctify you wholly and I pray, that your whole spirit, soul and body be presented blameless unto the coming of our Lord Jesus . 1 THESSALONIANS 5:23

Again in the book of Hebrew, we are told that:

The word of God is quick and powerful and is shaper than any two-edged sword, piercing even to the dividing asunder of soul and spirit. HEBREWS. 1:2

The enemy is cunning enough to know how to build these strongholds and where to build them. There are three areas in mankind in which these barriers can be constructed. These are in the spirit realm, the soulish realm and the physical realm.
As stated earlier, the Hebrew word for spirit is Ruach and the Greek word is Pneuma and both mean an invisible force . So of the types of spirit, we have God s personal spirit, which is the highest, then we have the Holy Spirit, angelic beings, and then there are Cherubim and the spirit of man. Lower down the line we have spirit of antichrist and demonic spirits.

THE SPIRIT OF MAN

This is the highest part of the tripartite being, and is the part that is capable of linking up and communicating with God, the father.

When Adam and Eve were created, they were closely connected with God, could hold conversations with him and visibly see Him. In the book of Genesis it is clear that their spirit man was more functional.

And the Lord called unto Adam. And Adam said unto Him, I heard thy voice in the Garden and was afraid because I was naked. GENESIS 3: 9

It was through disobedience that man fell from grace and was cast from the Garden of Eden. Sin then became rampant in his life. The Lord says in Genesis 6:3:

My spirit shall not always strive with man.

As such, since the fall, Man has had a yearning to come back into the presence of God.

The spirit therefore being the highest in the tripartite being is comprised of the intellect, will, desires and conscience.

Consequently we pray in the spirit, sing in the spirit and because man is so far removed from the Lord, Jesus told us when He was departing form this world, that He would send us another comforter, which is the Holy Spirit. (St John. 14:26)

With this wonderful spirit, believers now have access to the throne of Grace. Paul tells us in the book of Romans that

The spirit helps us with our infirmities .
He says that:

We know not what to we should pray for, but the spirit maketh intercession for us. ROMANS 8: 26

The Holy Spirit reaches the Father where the spirit of man is unable to do, and prays for us when we do not know exactly what we should be praying for.

It is such a wonderful privilege to know that we have a comforter and a mediator who can reach God when we are unable to do so. What an awesome privilege.

THE SOULISH REALM

As said earlier, the soul and the spirit of man are immortal and are so closely related that it is sometimes quite difficult to separate them and to show different functions. Paul however has shown us differences in 1 Corinthians 2 verse 11and Hebrew 4 verse twelve, and David in the Book of psalm103 and verse 104.

The bible speaks of the soul as being: Hungry, proverbs. 6:3. Weary, [Job10: 1, Jer.4: 31]. Empty. [Is. 29: 8]. Love, [Deut.6: 5]. Bitter, [1Sam.30: 6]. Referred to as the heart and as being oppressed, [Ex. 23: 9,Lev. 29: 16]. And as being proud, [Prob. 28: 25]. As the mind, being affected, rejoicing and as having desires [Deut.28: 65].

THE BODY

This is the container for both the soul and the spirit. The bible tells us that the body is the temple of the spirit [1Cor.3: 16], And that saints ought to glorify God in It.[1Cor.6 :20].

It is the only part of the tripartite man which dies at physical death, the soul and the spirit live on.[Josh. 2 :26]. The body ought to be made a living sacrifice for Jesus. It is the temple of Christ and therefore should be kept free of sinful pollution, which include fornication and adultery.

HOW DOES SATAN BUILD THESE STRONGHOLDS IN MEN?

If we recall what has been discussed regarding the spirit of man, we will remember that Man communicates with God through prayer, worship and praise. Satan, our defeated foe would like to praise the Lord with us, but he just cannot because his pride caused him to be separated from God. He is now defeated and is therefore unable to reach him.

We can be certain that Satan knows how pleasant it is to worship the Lord, as he too used to do this, along with the many other angels in heaven. As he is now unable to do this his desire to draw us into his kingdom is compounded by his envy of our praises and subsequent endeavours to hinder us from worshipping God.

How many times have you wanted to pray and worship the Lord but felt as if you are unable to do so? Because your spirit includes your feelings, Satan will often work in this area to try to build strongholds of weakness in your spirit.

Another example is when you are filled with the Holy Spirit. God gives you a beautiful language that Satan cannot understand. Furthermore, he is afraid when he hears your Holy Tongues, because they pour out of the wounds of Jesus. They come through the blood.

Without the shed blood of Jesus, there would be no comforter. Satan knows that, and he knows that that is one language that he just cannot speak. What he will do is try to prevent you from speaking, or, as soon as you do speak, he will try to prevent you from speaking your language again. In this way he will try to build a stronghold against the functioning of the Holy Spirit in your life and tell you that your tongues sound wrong.

As we know, Satan is a liar and the author of all lies. Bind him in the name of Jesus and speak that beautiful language! For as soon as you do begin to speak, then he will have to go.

Your language is one thing that reminds him so much of Calvary. It reminds him of the blood and the victory at the cross, when the Lord descended into hell, shamed him in front of his spooks and snatched the keys of hell and of death from him.

The tongues remind him of his future, that he has none. For a person who has a future of a thousand years in chains followed by eternal damnation, certainly has no future.

On the Holy Spirit, the bible further says that:

For the Holy Spirit Makes Intercession For you, With Groaning that Just Cannot Be Uttered.

Sometimes you might be fellowshipping at church, and suddenly a feeling of complete hopelessness takes over the whole service. You want to worship, but the place feels as though it has just fallen under a ton of bricks.

This is another example of how the enemy tries to build strongholds in your mind to hinder the Holy Spirit from operating. The enemy is so crafty that sometimes the service can be so charged with the presence of dark forces that if you are not careful, you will just take your bag and walk out.

We give thanks that the bible tells us that:

Where sin abound grace will much more abound. Romans 5:20

In these circumstances, the leadership should always take authority in the name of Jesus, bind those demons and allow the Holy Spirit to move.

The bible tells us that one will chase a thousand and that two will put ten thousand to flight. If there were only two of you in that building, you would represent ten thousand. So what about a church of two hundred saints? If you did not take the authority and begin to worship God with everything that is within you, call down the Glory of God in the temple, and kick those demons out, you would never receive a break through.

God Himself can see when those demons are gathering around, and through Him you have the power to summon ten thousand angels to take authority over the situation, to bind them and to cast them back into hell. Those evils are no match for God s mighty angels, for where sin abound, grace will much more abound.

But those angels will not be summoned until you begin to take authority over those forces of darkness. You must begin to move by faith and begin to tear down every fortress of the enemy, every barricade, every wall of fortification. Begin to move under the anointing of the Holy Spirit, and move those demons out.

You have the authority to do so. God has empowered you and has armoured you with weapons that are not carnal. As I have mentioned before, this is not physical warfare, grenades can t fight the enemy, and you cannot go into an aeroplane and drop physical bombs upon them. Noise can t kill them, neither can you slap them nor can you kick them.

But when you are armoured up with the word of God, and you put on the name of Jesus, remember that you are now a child who is washed in the blood of the Lamb. The Spirit of God also sanctifies you, therefore when you begin to wage war in the Spirit. God will draw back the curtains of brass from over our heads and will begin to drop some spiritual guerrilla bombs into the enemy s camp.

He will then place a spiritual sword in your hand and you will begin to chop in the spirit, kick in the spirit, thump in the spirit and every spiritual stronghold will have to be broken. So we put to flight demon powers and alien armies. We nullify the plan of the enemies and anything that exalts itself against the knowledge of God.

When we raise high the banner of Jesus Christ, then we are raging spiritual warfare against the kingdom of darkness and we are pulling down strongholds. But we cannot use unclean weapons neither can they be fleshy, but rather mighty spiritual weapons.

BREAKING STRONGHOLDS IN THE SOULISH REALM

Strongholds in the soulish realm along with those in the realm of the spirit t can go as far back to the time of your conception. Many children have been born to teenage parents who would not have been prepared for motherhood, and who would have subsequently rejected their baby from the time of conception. Furthermore, some of us just were not bought up in the pew and have been exposed to the world from a very young age.

Many young parents have taken the step of giving up their babies for adoption at birth, while grandparents and extended members of the family have assisted with the upbringing of others.

Some would have remained with mothers who had rejected them, while some parents openly tell their children that it was a mistake having them. Still there is another set who are raised in environments of physical, sexual, and drug abuse. These circumstances will inevitably place negative attitudes and behavioural patterns in the soulish realm.

We must understand that Satan and his demons are not always responsible for our fear, failures and problems in life. Of course there are times when we must go into spiritual warfare to deal with strongholds in our lives. But we must know when we are dealing with soulish strongholds, which have nothing to do with demonic forces.

In these instances we can bind and loose, cast out principalities, and break down fortresses from now until eternity. Until we identify the areas of our unsurrendered soul, which need to be surrendered and submitted to the will of God, we will continue to find ourselves hurting, unhealed, financially, socially, morally, spiritually and otherwise stagnated.

We must learn how to submit our will, our thoughts, our ways, our attitudes, and our minds, and in fact our entire life to the Lord.

Let s say that you were sexually abused as a child. Through this abuse, you might find that you have developed a fear of communicating with members of the opposite sex and will consequently have difficulties in forming a meaningful relationship.

This is a stronghold of fear and also that of rejection, which has been developed in the realm of the soul, and does not have to be associated with demons. You should go into warfare prayer during which time you take the authority and break those strongholds from your lives. You should command that every stronghold of rejection and fear that has been formed in the realm of the soul be broken and that you be loosened from those hurt and pain that you have been carrying around with you for years.

You should ask the Lord to assist you in overcoming that apprehension so that you can have healthy relationships. You can bind and loose demons as much as you like, but where there is no demon to expel, none will leave. This is an area of your soul that you should fast and pray about.

However there can be different circumstances, for example when you find that you are having sexual intercourse in your sleep and that you are frequently experiencing itching and burning in your sexual organs. If there is no proof that you have a diagnosed infection, then you would have had an evil spirit, which came into your womb, for the ladies and the testicles for the men at the time of the rape or other sexual intercourse. This is what we call a spirit transfer.

Most people who commit rape are transporting with them this sort of unclean lust spirit, which they can easily pass on through their sperm and this nastiness will remain with you and will only leave through a proper deliverance service. I believe that every individual who has been sexually abused should receive deliverance.

It is because of this transfer of spirit that most of these individuals will go on to commit rape because they are transporting this evil lust spirit with them. Ask many individuals who have been abused and they will tell you if they are honest that they either feel like doing it to others, or that they have actually done it to someone else.

OPEN DOORWAYS

This abuse can also leave you with what is called in the deliverance ministry, and open door of sin. It is through these doors that these evils which are called socubus and incubus spirits can enter and leave your bodies at will and will have sexual intercourse with you. In the case of a sexual open door, this will inevitably lead to fibroids, frequent miscarriages, and eventual cancer of the womb in the case of the ladies and prostate cancer in the case of the man.

Ladies with these open doors in their lives can sometimes have very horrible menstrual flow. Many are unable to conceive and when they do they will lose the child prematurely if they did not receive deliverance.

Sometimes this problem can be associated with a curse, which has been placed on the woman through a jealous lover of the husband or some other evil persons. Whichever way it comes, curses can only come through open doors and therefore this should be treated in the same manner as casting out a demon that has entered through sexual abuse.

I have seen where many writers have written on the topic of open doorways without fully understanding what these are and how they come about. There are basically two types of open doors, one is that which has been opened as a result of sin, the next is that which is associated with the organs of the body and through which an individual can be afflicted by the forces of darkness. I will deal with the latter here.

In the world of witchcraft, occultists, psychics and other witches take time to study what they call chackra in the human body. These are what they call the energy points and are areas through which they can hurt their victims.

These chackras would begin from the crown of the head, and run the length of the body along the region of the spinal cord and are associated with some major glands. There are generally seven of these, beginning with the pituary gland. If, for example, witches want to curse someone in the head, they would begin here and cast their spells around this area.

One of these chackras are located at the centre of what they call the third eye, where the eyebrows meet and where Hindu ladies often have some demonic mark.

I have learnt that in some cultures, rituals are performed to make a slit in this area of the body and that a demonic object is placed there. This it is assumed gives the individual powers to see into the realm of darkness and to perform witchcraft. In London it is a common thing to meet individuals with this awful looking engravement of an additional eye located at this area where the eyebrows meet.

Other energy points are said to be located at the throat, in the heart cavity, the stomach area, below the navel, at the rectum and at the bottom of the foot. According to these occultists, it is through these regions of the body that you can receive and lose energy and although I have never practised any of these methods, I am sure that the victims of the wicked ones can be badly damaged through these areas. In their world of darkness, witches are specifically trained how to protect these areas.

In occultic terms, these are doorways and it is through these areas that demons enter and leave the body. Witches generally do long incantations and rituals to do so called covering of these areas. However, as born again Christians we do not have to be on guard to cover chackras for we know that the redeemed blood of Jesus constantly covers us from every attack of the enemy.

If however after a person has been delivered and should they find that they still have problems with fears phobias, unclean sexual desires of homosexuality, lesbianism or occultism, then they should go down in fasting and prayer to break ungodly soul ties from spirit realm.

These are ties that have been made with unclean forces in the realm of the spirit some of which are done knowingly and some unknowingly. Whichever form they take, they are very dangerous and therefore all strongholds of ungodly ties have to be broken.

You need to ask the Lord to sever every link between yourself and the realm of darkness, between your soul and theirs and between your spirit and theirs.

A stronghold can be an inherent sin, and can come in the form of a curse. In the case of a hereditary sin, we find that many family members will struggle with the same stronghold. In my own example, I remember that when I was a young child, I often heard of my eldest sister who was so great at telling the future that her home was always packed with people who wanted to consult her.

I had proven this for myself one day when she had come to visit us when I was a teenager. A friend of mine had been to visit me and shortly after he had left, she asked for him and told us that he should not have gone as he was about to have a nasty accident. This is exactly what happened, and furthermore someone was actually killed in that accident.

When I grew up, I found myself doing exactly what my sister was doing. At first I thought that it was great as the fame and money came my way. Shortly afterwards,

I realised that I had inherited a spirit of divination. This is both a stronghold and an inherited curse that was passed to me through my bloodline.

It took a lot for me to really break that generational curse and to get that familiar spirit out of me, and I am still praying for my sister. She still seems under the delusion that she has a gift, as is the case of so many people who possess this kind of evil spirit. The devil has his way of fooling them into believing that they have something very special.

For those of you who are reading this book and have these evils speaking through you, let me warn you in no uncertain terms that what you have are unclean spirits, which can only lead you to a dreadful and disastrous end.

This voice or voices that you are hearing is not the voice of the Lord. Neither are they those of angels. I have heard voices of evil, those of angels and that of the Lord, and I can agree with the songwriter who says:

> His voice makes a difference,
> When He speaks He relieves my troubled mind
> It s the only voice I hear that makes a difference.

The voice of Jesus is a gentle soothing voice. The voice of the enemy is rough and threatening. The voice of the Lord is healing and straightforward, and when He speaks, you hear one distinctive voice.

The enemy s voice is mixed up. It is as if you hear many voices speaking through one body, telling you all sorts of lies in a quick, sharp and often distorted manner.

When the Lord speaks to you He generally sends a witness, as the bible says, Out of the mouth of two or three

God will always send another person to bear witness with you while the devil can only send another demon to lie to you. God will never tell you destructive, lying and slanderous things about another individual. If a person needs your help, the Lord will point him/her in your direction. The bible tells us that the devil is the father of lies.

Our main responsibility therefore is to ensure that we serve the Lord with all our heart, with our soul, and with our mind and that we are not engaging in sin because sin is the Christian s open door through which demons can enter his life.

In truth, chackras are not just energy points, but rather the weak areas of your bodies through which demons can enter your life.

As Christians we know that we do not have to partake in any rituals involving endless demonic chanting and candle burning in order to get unclean spirits to do anything for us. For how can darkness shed light into darkness? This is totally impossible.

Once we are under the blood of Jesus then we are free from these attacks. We have no time to be covering specific areas because the blood of Jesus was shed that our tripartite man can be covered and be protected until the day of Jesus Christ. So we have no fear for the unfruitful works of darkness.

Remember that it is in the soulish realm that the devil builds some strongholds, and generally in the mind. The mind is his battleground, and the soul is the seat of all activities. Let s say for example that you sat with a friend and watched a pornographic film. Now while you were watching the film, you were entertaining the devil. So he sat and watched it with you.

After seeing that film, your mind will become fixed on the sexual immoralities that you saw and soon you ll find that you want to see more and more pornographic movies. So you might purchase one and then another and another.

As time goes by you will become so consumed with these movies that you may find yourself being addicted to them. Moreover, even if you want to stop doing this you can t, because the devil has built a stronghold in your life, and even though you may try your hardest to stop looking at these films you just can t get away from them.

Strongholds are emotional, physical, spiritual and psychological fortifications that the enemy uses to bind us, thus hindering us from worshipping God, hearing from Him, achieving our goals, and from expressing love. They hinder our formation of meaningful relationships and cause us to be afraid and to be in panic.

A stronghold can manifest itself as a very bad habit, which is extremely difficult to break, and can continue with you until it becomes very damaging and destructive. It is based on the strength of the wall that the enemy places around this area of sin in your life.

A person with a stronghold can behave as though an unclean spirit possesses him, when in fact what s/he has, is a bad habit in the spirit realm, which has not been surrendered to the Lord and which becomes an ungodly soul tie.

A born again, blood washed child of God cannot be possessed with an unclean spirit. If a person should profess that he /she is a Christian and is carrying an unclean spirit, then something is wrong with his Christian living. He has what you would call an unsurrendered soul tie, which needs to be destroyed. An ungodly soul tie is an open door of sin, which will allow the enemy to come into your life. If a stronghold goes unnoticed and undealt with, it can allow entry to an unclean spirit in your life.

I am frequently asked whether an unclean spirit can dwell in the life of a Christian. The answer is simple. Jesus will not share house with the devil. If you are a born again Christian, then you should have no open door of sin in your life or the devil will come in. When the devil comes in and if you choose to make him your master, then Jesus will go out.

The bible says that when an unclean spirit departs from a person it wanders around and cannot find any abiding city, then it will return to see if there is room in his former house. Should he find a vacancy, then he will go in search of others and they will come and dwell there and the last state of a man is worst than the first. Evil spirits cannot enter the life of a holy, righteous, blood washed child of God.

Chapter 15

Identifying an Unclean Spirit

And He asked him, 'What is thy name?' And he answered saying, 'my name is legion for we are many.' St Mark 5:9

PLAYING WITH YOUR MIND

If a patient is ill and goes to the doctor, the doctor would not automatically assume that the person has cancer, needs to be operated on, or that he is diabetic. Most doctors will know the symptoms that are associated with certain illnesses, although he may run certain tests.

While there are churches in which the term deliverance should not be used, in the same light there are others that over-emphasise the existence of demons. If their members have a head-ache, then they have a demon. If they have influenza, it is a demon of flu. If they have bad attitude and do not know when to keep quiet, they have a spirit of speaking. If it is a habit of drinking it is a spirit of drinking, and the list goes on. They are consumed with thoughts of the devil.

We must be able to identify the symptoms of a person before beginning to bind and loose. We cannot bind a devil that does not exist; neither can we loose a person from himself. We cannot see evil spirits but they can be discerned and the person carrying them will show signs of being possessed.

During one of our deliverance sessions a Somalian lady, who was also a Muslim was standing in the front row. As I looked at her from the corner of my eyes I noticed that she had a smirky expression on her face. When I looked at her fully, she had this horrible smile all over face, which looked very evil. I had a word of knowledge that she was possessed with unclean spirits. As soon as I ordered the demons to leave her she began to manifest. She fell on the floor and was screaming, sweating and rolling over as though she was in pain.

Demons are liars and we must not believe a word that they say. I continued to order them out telling them that they would harm no one that was present, and that they would go wherever the Lord sent them. I heard a funny voice came out in broken English with a Somalian accent, saying:
 Mi no speaky englishy.

I told those demons that they knew enough English to tell me that they didn t speak English and commanded him to keep quiet and to leave and so they did. This lady quickly picked up the bible and shouted:

They are gone! All of them! They are gone! I couldn t hold the bible before and now I can, they are gone!

She was ecstatically happy. She continued to explain that these evil spirits had tormented her life and had not allowed her to pick up the bible. She said that whenever she did, her hands shook so vigorously that she had to drop it.

HOW DEMONIC ACTIVITY IS MANIFESTED

1) Demons like to interfere with the central nervous system

    Remember the case of the demonic Gadarene. The evil spirits caused him to cut himself and to behave like a mad man.

    In today s society, the mental homes are filled with people who are under severe demonic oppression but who have been diagnosed as schizophrenic. When I was attacked, if it were not for the mercy of the Lord, I would have been thrown into a mental home to be treated for severe depression or some other form of mental disorder.

2) Demons will allow you to speak to yourself

    Demons will cause you to think all manner of insanity. In addition, they will drive you from place to place causing you to eat out of bins and living on the streets, just like so many of the people that we see wandering the streets. They do not like cleanliness and will allow you to live in a dirty unclean environment. Remember that the name Beelzebub, which is another name for Satan, means lord of the dunghill? A demon possessed person will be driven to live in a dunghill with the lord of the flies, and frequently when they appear to be speaking to themselves, they will, in fact, be speaking to demons.

3) Demons will speak from the inside of you

    Demonic voices will tell an individual all kinds of horrible thing such as:
     Go and kill yourself and finish with it .

You are nasty and dirty you are no good .

You belong to me, I now possess you.

4) Demons will often change your name so that you take on their s

One night as I was delivering a possessed young man, I heard a voice emerged from him that was not his own but was that of an older man. The voice said:

My name is not David my name is Jason. He belongs to me and you are a liar.

5) Demons can identify a born again Christian

Demons recognise born again Christians, and if they feel that you are about to deliver the person in whom they are dwelling, they will tell you lies like:

If you touch me I will kill myself.

If the person/s who is conducting deliverance does not understand what s/he is doing, they will believe that they are hearing from the victim, when in fact it is the demon speaking.

Other physical symptoms of those under demonic attack include the following:

6) Restlessness

Sometimes such persons cannot stay in one place for long and cannot keep still. They will have an uncontrollable urge to walk all over the place, itching and scratching themselves.

7) Eye Movements

Their eyes will flicker a lot and will move very fast.

8) Excessive Eating Habits

They will eat a lot because they are in fact feeding the evils in them.

9) Bloated Stomachs

Many times the victim s stomachs will be puffed up as this is the area in which these evils will sometimes take up their abode.

10) Headaches

They may have frequent headaches, and will suffer from tiredness and insomnia.

11) Exhaustion

They will often seem drowsy, sleepy, and restless.

They will speak of having many nightmares.

12) Excessive Strength

Often these individuals will demonstrate unusual strength and power.

13) Unstable Personalities

These people will often walk sluggishly and may show multiple personalities, have mood swings and be very aggressive.

14) Anti-social personalities

Their behaviour is often so anti- social that it becomes difficult for them to mix well with others.

Their lives are completely taken over and controlled by these demons and it is only the mercy of God that can set them free. These folks will seek help after a while because their lives will be very tormented and they will want to be free.

For some, the process of deliverance can be a very hard one as the individuals might have many smaller evils in them in addition to a mighty strong one, which generally controls the lesser ones. The petty ones are easy to get rid of but the high-powered controlling evil will be very stubborn. When the weaker ones leave, these strong ones will always get other ones to replace them.

I remember delivering a young man who had many unclean spirits in him. One night just after prayer service, he rang me from home to say that he had a strange experience. He said that as he was at home praying, he heard a rough course voice speaking in what was almost a growl, coming out of his own mouth. It said:

I am Accra and you belong to me.

By the grace of God, I had shortly before this incident held a discussion on how to deliver oneself, so when this voice surfaced the young man boldly told it that it had to leave his body because it did not belong there.

That man was so ill when he came to us that when I looked in his face, it was as though death was staring back at me. However when faced with the enemy, he took the authority in the name of Jesus and commanded those demons to leave him.

After his deliverance, he went to wash his face and he found that there were shreds, almost like flakes of ice emerging from under his skin. Further to this, he discovered knots of blue thread seeping out of his hands.

I explained to him that those were the demonic identification marks, which are like a form of tagging device. This can be compared with the tags that are given to prisoners who have not completed their sentences in prison. They are sent out with a tag , an electrical tracking device, which is connected to the police station. The alarm would be generated if the prisoner stays out past the allowed curfew.

The tags in this young man had identified him with the kingdom of darkness. They are like tracking devices that the enemy uses to find his victims. Generally after deliverance, they would melt or just disappear. In the case of this young man they melted.

Just recently, a lady came to me for deliverance. She had recently arrived in London from Zimbabwe. While I was taking her through deliverance, she showed me some big ugly batches of very dark circles that came out on her leg. I told her that they were inserts, explained to her what their functions were and told her that in a few days they would come up like boils then disappear. I also drew the attention of the team to these.

Unclean spirits are not things that we should play around with. Once they are identified, as deliverance Ministers we should not be cowards because God has not given us the spirit of fear, but one of love, of boldness, of power and of a sound mind. We must therefore take the authority and cast them out in the name of Jesus, for we are more than conquerors.

THE DELIVERANCE SERVICE

The deliverance Ministry is one, which seems to hold much fascination for many modern day preachers who from some of their writings seem to give the impression that they are mere exorcists. I believe that it is only an exorcist who would sit entertaining demons while they speak with them and tell them lies and foul languages.

Demons are liars and therefore we should not trust them to communicate with us. They are wicked and evil beings who will lie to you so that you might become exhausted during the course of the deliverance service.

The more they wear you out then the longer the service will take and if you allow yourself to get too tired, then they can overpower you. To find out the name of a demon is the most that is scriptural. Jesus did ask the demon in the demoniac of Gadarene, what his name was, and he told Him that his name was legions because there were so many demons dwelling there.

So yes, knowing the name of a demon or the type should help with the deliverance. However, there is nowhere in His earthly ministry where is it recorded that Jesus allowed demons to perform a comic show in front of Him. He spoke to them and they left.

We as Christians ought to be so armoured and sealed under the blood of Jesus to the extent that just merely saying the word forces evils to leave their victims.

Throughout this book, I have used my own experiences as a guide to illustrate how one should successfully conduct a deliverance. In summary we have shown that there are basically two sets of people who are involved in the process. These are:

a) The Person/s Conducting the Deliverance.

b) The Person/s to be delivered.

Any ordained woman or man of God that has the responsibility to cast out demons or to deliver someone from bondage is a deliverance minister. This is a very awesome and dangerous role and if someone is not called for this ministry and does not have the anointing on his/her life to do such work, he/she should not experiment with it. This is not an area of the ministry that one should experiment with.
I have lost two babies on this battlefield, but thanks be to God, the devil has won nothing for each trial has made me stronger. Also, I have learnt very important deliverance lessons during these times. In addition, I have taken ten steps up the spiritual ladder for each child, and I know that there are plenty more babies in

heaven for me, so the devil is a loser and so is his mother- in — law.

We are very precious to the Lord. He has entrusted a great ministry upon us and we should not be careless with it. We must abide in the throne room of Jesus Christ. We must spend quality time with the Lord praying and crying out for souls that are trapped in the Kingdom of darkness. God requires that we spend quality time on our knees in His presence.

Although we are born again Christians, it does not mean that we are all qualified to deliver souls from this type of darkness. Do not be fooled into thinking for one minute that Satan is happy to lose a soul out of his dark regime. He will do everything in His power to keep those poor souls in darkness. Therefore we will need to understand the tactics of the evil one.

Moreover, we are not called just to try to dethrone Christ by boasting about how many souls we are casting demons out of. If demons are cast out of unclaimed souls, which have not been sealed after their deliverance, then we are doing nothing less than increasing the suicidal and general death rate.

On an unsealed soul, the spirits will angrily and viciously go and get more vicious demons than themselves to possess the unclaimed and uncovered lives.

No one would be happy to let go off a thing that he has been holding on to for years let alone that which he has claimed to be his own. If a person has been in the camp of the enemy for a long time, then the devil has claimed ownership to that one and will not let go without a fight.

As Christians, and not just as deliverance ministers, our emphasis should not merely be based on earthly fame or empire building, it should be based on souls. We must have a hunger for souls. We must travail for souls like a woman in labour.

The prophet Isaiah asks the question:

Shall the earth be made to bring forth in one day? Or shall a nation be born at once?

He continues,

As soon as Zion travailed, she brought forth her children. Isaiah 66:8

We have one common foe, and that enemy has in bondage many of God s elect. It is therefore our responsibility to pray them out of Satan s hell.

In the book of Daniel chapter ten, we read where Daniel learnt from reading the prophecies of Jeremiah that it was nearing the time for the captured Jews to be released out of the Babylonian captivity. Having realised this, he began to pray to God for their release.

God requires that we as Christians awake from our slumber, move out of our comfort zone and begin to pray for the release of those that are in captivity. He does not only require that demons be removed from the lives of His children, but also that souls be born for the Kingdom of heaven and not only for End Time Ministry.

End Time is just a little peck in the bucket. What I desire is to claim souls for all the blood washed Churches of Jesus Christ.

One day we all are going to get to heaven where these ministries will cease to exist. And in their place will be one big banner bearing words such as these:

 These are they that have been through many trials, but have come out as gold; that have been through the furnace, and have been washed in the blood of the Lamb! These are THE REDEEMED OF CHRIST.

Oh what a day that will be when the saints are gathering in. This should be our duty as children of God. We must make sure that the saints of God are being gathered in. It is for such a reason that God is raising up deliverance ministries, to enable us to wage war against the kingdom of darkness and to get God s children out. We are not working for an earthly inheritance.

The apostle Peter tells us that :

We are begotten into a lively hope by the resurrection of Jesus Christ from the dead to an inheritance, incorruptible and undefiled and that which fadeth not away, reserved in heaven for us. 1 Peter.1:4

Therefore, because we know that we are not working for earthly pay we should subsequently make all the effort to do the will of the Lord. In addition, we should have at the top of our list, the responsibility to birth souls for the Kingdom of God, and so we daily travail for souls to be born for the kingdom of God.

We then have our team of prepared people who are ready to take on the hosts of hell. They should be righteous, blood-washed holy Ghost filled children of God with a renewed mind and who have been in fasting and prayer before the deliverance and who should break their fast before engaging the enemy.

The reason for this is that fasting can cause us to become physically drained and it is during these times that we are likely to be attacked. In addition, the deliverance might take longer than we had anticipated and this can further cause a stress upon your physical man. In all things, the Lord requires that we use wisdom. We ought to be as wise, or rather, wiser than, a serpent.

Before the deliverance, the team should get together and cover each other with prayer. If I were not doing a mass deliverance, then I would have met with the person or persons beforehand for counselling. Through the gift of discernment, I would, on most occasions, be able to tell what kind of spirits we are dealing with and would be able to prepare my team for this session. I would also be able to advise them of the tactics they should employ to cast such spirits out.

A pre- counselling session will also allow you to find out whether a session would take a long time or not. For example as stated before, some folks are quite happy to keep their demons.

Quite often, folks are driven to seek help because of the sufferings, which these wicked beings have inflicted upon them, others might have come out of mere curiosity, while some might just come to test your spirit. And believe me, they will be able to tell whether you are a clean spirit or not.

Remember how the demon that had possessed the life of the Gadarene man had quickly identified Jesus and instantly asked Him the question

What have I to do with thee, Jesus thou son of the most High God?

It continued:

I adjure thee by God that thou torment me not. St Mark 5:7.

They knew who Jesus was and, furthermore, they were afraid of Him. If you are not a prepared vessel, unclean spirits will be able to identify you. Moreover, instead of you dealing with them they will handle you as they did with the seven sons of Sceva of Acts 19.

When I was making my way out of darkness, a young lady came to see me who was possessed with several demons. It was at the time when I had just begun to lead souls to the Lord. I took this young woman to a church where I felt that she could receive her deliverance.

That night I sat in the church feeling very humiliated and angry as the evils took over the church. They jumped and danced around and were telling the ministers all sorts of horrible things.

It was like something out of a comedy show and people were laughing, as these things were being allowed to star the show. At one stage, the unclean spirit looked at the crew of born again Christians, including the pastor of the church and laughed at them. Then it began dancing and chanting:

Weaklings! Weaklings! Weaklings! Weaklings!

At one point, I was so angry that I felt like casting them out myself. However, I did not feel that I was ready at the time to do so and therefore I left them to continue with whatsoever they were doing. There was no way that those Christians could manage those things.

When delivering a victim, we usually make use of the consecrated olive oil, and I would like to comment in passing on the unholy use of perfumed oil. Perfumed oils, which are generally sold at the occult shop, the body shop, the aromatherapist or the herbalists, are very dangerous occultic tools and should be stayed clear off. They are usually chanted over by witches and are packed with demons. When they are used on individuals they usually leave a lingering scent, which attracts evil spirits to the users.

One could even use cooking oil to anoint the afflicted as along as it is consecrated, but please stay clear of the demon-possessed perfumed oils in the shops. We just cannot use darkness to fight darkness. We must use weapons that are not carnal.

Chapter 16

Conducting a Deliverance

How can one enter into a strong man's house, and spoil his goods, except he first bind the strong man? And then he will spoil his house. St Matthew 12:29.

PROTECTING THE INNOCENTS

As Christians, we need to understand that wherever the spirit of the Lord is there is liberty.

Deliverance can and does automatically take place in any Holy Ghost charged service. I have conducted many services, which were not deliverance based, but as soon as I began to preach the word of God, people would begin to manifest demons. I will not, if at all possible allow anyone to leave any of my services with an unclean spirit and, therefore, I will always take the authority to cast it out.

I have already explained how at one time unclean vessels were assigned to destroy my assembly and it was only by the good Grace of God that the individual left that meeting alive. The bible tells us that:

When the enemy shall come in like a flood, the spirit of the Lord shall set up a standard against him. ISAIAH 59:19

When the young man began to manifest those evils it was as though the breath was leaving his body and the Lord taught him a lesson in that place.

However, because of the intensity of this type of ministry, the uncleanness of the type of forces that we are dealing with and for the protection of others around, deliverance is best done away from a big congregation.

It can be a very frightening thing to be speaking to someone who appears to be a quite healthy and normal human being and suddenly hear another completely different voice coming from the person. This could be that of the opposite sex and in the case of the male is often very coarse, horrible sounding and threatening.

Although this can happen to small children, we would not want them to be exposed to such activities and most certainly would not allow them to have these sorts of fears and nightmares to deal with. In essence, children are very vulnerable and should be kept well away from these scenes. If it is necessary that they have to be there, then they should be covered with the blood of Jesus. They should be prayed over and anointed with oil. However, if it can be avoided, they should not be presented in the room in which the deliverance is taking place.

Sometimes we do not know what type of demon is presented in the person and although we command them to hold their peace and to leave, they will show their true form when they are leaving. For example, they might begin to behave just like a snake, crawling on the belly in a twisted manner, hissing and pushing out the tongue.

That is a snake spirit and one of the most dangerous. It is certainly one of the worst spirits and is usually present in those who have truly sold themselves to the devil. These are also those who have gone to seek occultic power. In return, this serpent would be working inside them for Lucifer. Others might belong to very high cults like the brotherhood of man.

In some cases people will begin to roar like a lion, bark like a dog or even to behave like a cat. As they begin to manifest these evils their whole countenance will change to resemble that of the creature being manifested. We should not encourage them to continue manifesting or to speak to us. Apart from telling you who they are, do not be entertained by unclean spirits. They should be asked to leave at once.

At the time of writing this book, a young lady came to see me for counselling. She had just recently been married and things had begun to go very wrong. The couple was at each other's throats and there was no peace in the relationship. When she came to see me, she was on the verge of walking out on her husband. She was in a lot of tears and she felt that there was no hope.

I counselled her, and during the session, I realised that she had a cobra spirit with her. This spirit was quite a nasty one and as soon as we started to deliver her, it began to hiss, to curl up and was crawling on the floor.

This was a most beautiful young woman and one who no one would expect to be walking around transporting a cobra spirit with her. It was quite easy for us to deliver her, as she really wanted to get rid of this evil thing and so she helped with her deliverance.

This young lady had gone into a secret cult believing that the members were true Christians. She told us that she was fascinated with the powers and opportunities that they were offering and felt that by joining the cult, she too would become powerful.

Even after she was delivered, there were backlashes. This woman had unconsciously entered a marital contract with this evil spirit, who was then making sure that she had no other relationship.

All her other relationships had failed and after her deliverance this demon returned to separate her from her husband. It was a fight to keep that union. This evil thing saw her as his property and was making sure that she did not form a meaningful relationship.

Given the nature of deliverance, therefore, it is both difficult and unfair to have cowards, babies and people who are weak, sick or frail around when all of this is happening. In cases like these, deliverance should include the person to be delivered and the deliverance ministers. If you are someone who uses praise and worship in your deliverance meetings, then your musicians should be born again Christians who are covered by the blood of Jesus.

STEP ONE: CONSECRATE THE DELIVERANCE AREA

The day before deliverance is to take place, I usually seal the place by applying consecrated oil to the doors, windows, across the doors and the walls of the house. In the process, I do conduct a consecration and dedication prayer. This is done to ensure that unclean spirits stay away from the premises and also that when they leave they do not return.

STEP TWO: HAVE AN INFORMAL DISCUSSION

Most of the people from End Time Healing Ministry have been delivered from some form of bondage. I find that it helps to have an informal chat with the person/s seeking deliverance, before commencing. We generally sit together and introduce ourselves, during which time we share experiences. This will allow people who have been delivered to speak freely and openly of the oppression that they had endured from the enemy, and the strongholds that they have overcome.

By the time we get around to the person/s in bondage, they would be feeling quite relaxed and eager to tell of what they were going through and why they had come. That will greatly clear the way for deliverance to take place and will allow the demons to understand that the individual is ready and in agreement with us, so that they should be prepared to vacate their bodies.

STEP THREE: PRAISE AND WORSHIP

I always begin my deliverance services with praise, prayer and worship. In so doing I invite the presence of the Holy Spirit within the place. This is important because the oppressed usually carry with them a very heavy spirit of oppression. It is not strange to walk into a deliverance room and feel as though the place is so claustrophobic that you feel in need of room to breathe. This is generally due to the presence of the legions that have been hounding the person or persons to be delivered.

The atmosphere should be charged with the presence of the Holy Spirit before conducting this service. This will make the process much easier for everyone concerned. I have had praise and worship services during which demons began to manifest before the actual deliverance could take place. Moreover, while we ignore the possessed person and continue with our worship we afterwards realised that we had no need to proceed further with the deliverance as by then the demons would have left.

STEP FOUR: SPEAKING THE WORD

After our praise, we enter a period of collective prayer and worship, during which time we would make use of the name of Jesus, the blood of Jesus and the power of the Holy Ghost, and would apply the word of God.

We would speak with authority, the logos word and allow it to become rhema to us. We remind ourselves that We are more than conquerors, and that God has not given us the spirit of fear, but of power and of love and of a sound mind.

We declare that God has given us the power to tread on scorpions and on serpents, and that what we bind on earth has already been bound in heaven and that what we loose on earth will also have bee loose in heaven.

STEP FIVE: THE POWER IN THE NAME

Having charged our atmosphere with praise, prayer, and worship, the deliverance service would be well on its way. I have read in some books where writers have indicated that a deliverance service should not be done by a group of people, but rather by one person at a time. I have no problem with that, if that works well for them, then that s fine.

However, the bible tells us that one shall put a thousand to flight and that two shall put ten thousand to flight. (ISAIAH 30: 17).

When one is worshipping in a congregation that is filled with anointed people and with the presence of the Holy Spirit, as soon as the worshippers begin to collectively send up the praises to God one can automatically feel the atmosphere being charged with the presence of the Holy Spirit. Moreover, in that service we quite often witness an awesome anointing, which allows all sorts of miracles to take place.

In our services, we collectively take authority over the forces of darkness and ask them to leave in the name of Jesus. Jesus never walked with His disciples so as to be sure that they would be able to do the work if He were not able to. He had them with Him to teach them spiritual truth, so that the work of the Kingdom would continue until the Lord put in His appearance.

It generally takes more than one service for deliverance to effectively take place. Most demonised people are traumatised from their experiences and will demand a lot of highly specialised love, care, and support for a long time. Therefore, the casting out of the demons just will not complete deliverance. In fact, this is only the beginning.

Jesus taught us to command evil spirits to leave in His name, and as such, during the deliverance, we boldly command demons to leave in the name of Jesus. While some are commanding them to leave, others will be pleading the blood of Jesus, while deliverance songs are being played in background. Other members of the group who are not directly involved with the deliverance or those who are not as experienced, will be sending up the glory and the praises to the Lord while the service is taking place.

We often let demons know that they will leave and that they will go where the Lord sends them. We let them know that while they are leaving, they will harm no one, for each person is covered by the blood of Jesus.

STEP SIX: REBUKE THE ENEMY AND GIVE GOD THE GLORY

When the evils are leaving the bodies of the oppressed. You will sometimes hear them gurgling or choking as though the breath was leaving the body. They will sometimes look pale and very weak and might froth at the mouth. If an animal spirit has been presented in the individual, then s/he will begin to manifest that demon.

Some demons will show signs of stubbornness and as stated earlier, they may try to hold conversations with you. Rebuke them in the name of Jesus! Apart from knowing the type of demon that you are dealing with, you are not a medium, and you will not listen to the lies and schemes of the wicked one. Remember, you are in charge, and not some spooks from hell!

Whenever you notice the signs outlined above, do not retreat, do not call for the paramedics, and do not give up. Those are very good signs that you are in fact winning the battle and it means that you are near the end of that deliverance. Soon you will notice that all the commotion has ended and the individual comes around as though s/he has just arrived from another planet.

Sometimes they might feel very hungry, as some of them might not have eaten for a very long time. Some might feel very thirsty and should be given a drink. We must always be mindful that these people have just been through a battle and will be spiritually sore as those spooks ripped their way through their bodies to leave. Pray for their healing and handle them with care and compassion. In most cases, s/he is unaware of the extent of the battle that they have just been through and will seem very relaxed and quite composed.

Begin to give God the Glory for the battle that has just been won. Only a deliverance minister and those who are directly involved in this type of ministry can tell you of the joy and peace that they feel deep within their spirits, after they have delivered someone from the kingdom of darkness.

To know that deliverance has been granted to a life that has been taken and been used and abused; that has been battered and beaten. A life from which all hope had gone, that was slowly going out like the wick of a burning candle, melting away before one s eyes, with no hope and a future in darkness, and that it could have been retrieved from the kingdom of darkness to give God the Glory!

This is one of the greatest part of the plan of salvation. To take the kingdom of darkness by force and to redeem God s children, from Satan s slave market.

STEP SEVEN: POST DELIVERANCE COUNSELLING

The delivered person has just been through a tough battle. A battle that can leave them very traumatised for a long time. Many will be still asking the question: Lord why me? Many of them were merely victims, who didn t take part in any agreement to have Satan using his evil ones to possess their lives.

These people often see themselves as being dirty and corrupt and will want to compare themselves with other Christians, believing that they will never be like them.

The last thing that they want is for their stories and pictures to be all over the front page of a Christian magazine. As pastors it is our responsibility to be sensitive to those who are in our care. If these people want to share their testimonies with others, then the Lord will guide them into doing so. The last thing that they need is further humiliation at the hands of a pastor whose only desire may be to take the glory for himself.

Our role is now to counsel them and read encouraging scriptures with them. We need to give them positive words of advice, which should include the importance of filling that vacuum with the love of Jesus, because we do not want any unclean spirits to return to their lives. We should pay these people regular visits to make sure that they continue with their Christian walk.

The first few weeks after their deliverance are very important ones. These are the times when the unclean forces generally lurk around the delivered individuals. Their desire is to return to squat in their bodies. The delivered person/s will need the presence of the Lord around them very much.

Shortly After deliverance, I generally hold tarrying services for the infilling of the Holy Spirit. I am always aware that those are the times when these folks need a comforter. What greater comforter there is, than the Holy Spirit?

The bible tells us in the book of St. Luke that:

There is joy in heaven over one sinner that repenteth, more than over ninety and nine just persons, which need no repentance. Luke 15:7

Since I began to seek souls for the kingdom of heaven I have witnessed many battered and bruised souls who have returned to the Lord in humbleness and in their brokenness.

I have seen the Lord change the drug addict into a preacher, I have seen Him change a high Priest from the Kingdom of darkness into a vessel of honour for Himself. Folks who were hooked on tarot phone lines have become great Missionaries for Christ. Occultists have been changed and many lives that have been tormented and ruined by the forces of darkness have found peace, happiness, tranquillity, comfort and restoration in the caring arms of Jesus.

This is the plan of salvation, that God's children should return to the shepherd and bishop of their souls. That we as children of God should take a stand for righteousness, and for holiness and redeem those that are lost and wounded and offer to them God's plan for their lives. There is greater rejoicing in heaven over one sinner that needs repentance than over ninety and nine just persons who need no repentance.

God is happy in glory, when His children return unto Him, when we try to walk in His pathway and endeavour to do the things that are pleasing in His sight.

God wants us as His children to have a yearning within us, for souls for His Kingdom. I remember one day, bowing in the presence of the Lord as I travailed for souls to be born for His Kingdom.

During that time, I was preparing for a baptismal service, and as I knelt there in the presence of the Lord, I began to ask myself the question:
I wonder if I am doing what is pleasing to the Lord.

Suddenly I had a vision of a choir of angels, which came and sat around me as I was lost in praise and worship and they folded their wings. Then I heard a voice saying:

The Lord is well pleased with you my child.

I just want you to know that when you honour the Lord and do His will with all that is within you, then he will take care of you. When He gives a order and you do what He tells you to do, then he will walk with you. When we go out there and look for the souls that are under bondage and those that are demonised and loose them from those shackles and grave clothes, then the Lord will bless us. When we call them to the Kingdom of God, then our father will be well pleased with us.

I know that many of you who are reading this book might be wondering whether demons are real or whether they are just figments of our imagination. I just want you to know that I am writing mainly from my own experience and not from what I have read in some books.

Not only do they exist but also I can also confirm that they are very wicked, and that they are here to kill, to steal, and to destroy. In addition, they are no respector of persons.

We tend sometimes in our ignorance to laugh at folks who are under oppression, to see them as inferior beings, and sometimes we almost take the attitude of the Pharisee towards them. It s as if we say to ourselves:

Thank God that I am not like those ones, I am a much better person than they are. Since they are acting so stupid I do not even want to associate myself with them, and I certainly have no time for them.

The fact is, none of us in life knows what will befall us. Therefore, if we see someone suffering from oppression, if we do not understand what he or she is going through or what is happening to him or her, then we should not scorn them, and nor should we ridicule them or say anything unpleasant about them. The truth is that it could be you and you just do not know what that person is undergoing.

It is easy to identify a person who is demonised. However there is another set of poor souls who have been overlooked and ignored and these people can sometimes be in a worst position than the possessed ones. These are those who have fallen prey to a curse or spell.

This is an area, which is often overlooked in the deliverance ministry and one on which I would like to focus in the following chapter.

Chapter 17

Spells & Curses

Moreover all these curses shall come upon thee and shall pursue thee and overtake thee till thou be destroyed. Because thou harkenedest not unto the voice of the Lord thy God to keep His commandments and His statues which He commanded thee. Deuteronomy 28: 45

UNDERSTANDING CURSES

The word curse is taken from the Greek word **katara**, which means intensive, down, execration, imprecation, or something that is uttered out of malevolence. It is also used by God to pronounce righteous judgement. When used as a verb it means **anathematizo** and means devoted to destruction, accursed, or to bind by a curse. It is also used in the sense of the verb **kakologeo**, which means to speak evil of.

I would like us to briefly examine the word curse in the sense of the Greek word Katara above and as used by God in pronouncing judgement.

In a previous chapter, we looked at strongholds in detail. We were told that these are spiritual fortifications that are generally used by the evil one to bind a person. They are used to keep the truth from reaching us and to set up constant attacks against us.

As such one of the constant messages in this book is that we must put on the whole armour of God. It is with our armour on and in place that we are able to identify and deal with strongholds.

Curses can be inherited and can come down through the bloodline in the form of generational curse. I would like to briefly examine some of these curses from a biblical view point which include rape, incest, drug abuse, polygamy, rejection and murder, and expose how they can affect one s spiritual growth and success in life.

THE GENERATIONAL CURSE OF MURDER

And in process of time it came to pass, that Cain brought of the fruit of the ground an offering unto the Lord. And Abel brought of the firstlings of his

flock and of the fat thereof. And the Lord had respect unto Abel and unto his offering. But unto Cain and his offering He had not respect. And Cain was very wroth and his countenance fell. GENESIS. 1: 3-5

And Cain talked with Abel his brother and it came to pass that when they were in the field, that Cain rose up against Abel his brother and slew him. VERSE 8

And the Lord said unto Cain where is Abel thy brother? And he said, I know not: Am I my brother s keeper? And He said what hast thou done? The voice of thy brother s blood crieth to me from the ground. And now hast thou cursed from the earth, which hath opened her mouth to receive thy brother s blood. When thou tillest the ground it shall not henceforth yield unto thee her strength; A fugitive and vagabond shalt thou be in the earth. VERSES 9 -12

Here the bible shows us one of the worst scenes of evil, jealousy, covetousness, and envy, all of which result in murder. Cain was jealous of his brother because he had given God a more acceptable gift than he had, and because of this he killed his only brother.

God then placed a curse upon him and cast him from His presence, after which he became a vagabond upon the earth. Therefore, we have inherited the Canaanite spirit of murder and deadly covetousness, of jealousy and of envy. It is no wonder that we hear of so many family members who have killed their relatives in cold-bloodedness. Nations are at war with nations and are destroying each other over what could be described as a morsel of bread.

Even in our churches there is so much envy and jealousy. You find that there are people in churches who refuse to be servants for Christ. Everyone wants to be a leader. Everyone wants to be the next important person. There are more healers in churches now than there are chair for folks to sit on.

Sisters have to be like sisters, brothers like brothers. The stronghold and curse of jealousy have taken control of their lives. Jealousy is amongst the worst form of evil. Therefore, we should break that along with the others that have been mentioned from the bloodline.

We call those, the Canaanite curses, which are meant to keep us down. These hinder us from being obedient and from waiting upon the Lord for our share of blessing. Some folks prefer to kill than to wait on the Lord.

I am confident that had Cain waited upon the Lord and had he tried again, then the Lord would have accepted his offering the next time around. However, he was unable to wait because the jealousy in him was too overwhelming. He had a thirst for blood. Many of our young women and men are going around with this Canaanite spirit, thirsty for their brothers and sisters blood.

BREAKING CANAANITE CURSES

We break that curse from out of the bloodline in the name of Jesus. We take authority over every curse of Cain, of jealousy and envy of murder and of covetousness. We take authority over them and we cast them out of our generation. We break that curse going back to twenty generations in the name of Jesus!

THE GENERATIONAL CURSE OF INCEST

And Lot went up out of Zoar, and dwelt in the mountains and his two daughters with him: For he feared to dwell in Zoar. And he dwelt in a cave he and his two daughters. And the first born said unto the younger our father is old, and there is not a man in the earth to come in unto us after the manner of all the earth. Come let us make our father drink wine, and we will lie with him, that we may preserve seed for our father.

And they made their father drunk that night and the firstborn went in and lay with her father, and he perceived neither when she lay down nor when she arose.

And it came to pass on the morrow, that the first born said unto the younger, Behold I lay yesternight with my father; Let us make him drink wine this night also and go thou in and lay with him that we may preserve seed of our father.

And they made their father drink wine that night also and the younger arose, and lay with him and he perceived not when she lay down nor when she arose. Thus were the children of Lot with child by their father. And the firstborn bare a son and called his name Moab and the same is the father of the Moabites unto this day. And the younger she also bare a son and called his name Benamni. The same is the father of Ammon unto this day. GENESIS 19:30—38

God had taken Lot and his family out of the city of Sodom and the bible tells us that as they were on their way out, his wife looked back and became a pillar of salt.

It was customary in those days for the first-born boy to become heir of the property. However, as we read in the scriptures, Lot had no male child. What we see therefore is the incestuous picture of Lot s daughters making him drunk, sleeping with him and becoming pregnant. This has to be one of the worst examples of incest that has ever been recorded.

The bible goes on to tell us that the girls had two sons. The first was named Moab and is derived from the Hebrew **Mowab** which means from my father. The other child was named Benamini from the Hebrew **Ammon**, or son of my people. It is from these tribes that we have the Ammonites and the Moabites. These are among the tribes that God later sent the Israelites to conquer and to take the land from.

They were idolatrous people and those that the Lord had warned His people against, however instead of destroying them as the Lord had told the Israelites to do, they slept with them and had children with them. As such, it is no wonder that the curse of incest and rape is so common in some households.

Actually every day that we turn on our televisions, or the radio, or look in the papers, we hear and read of such horrific stories of molestation and abuse in the family that they make us sick. Many of our folks are scarred for life because of some form of horrible abuse that they had suffered at the hands of their uncles, aunts, fathers, stepfathers and parents and other family members.

Many folks take this anger, hatred, resentment and feelings of rejection throughout their lives into the work situations and marriages. Some never seek counselling, but rather keep their anger bottled up inside of them. Many partners have ended up realising after their wedding day that their partners are carrying emotional baggage and many of these relationships do fail.

Many of our women and men who should have been in the churches have become lesbians and homosexuals; some have become drug addicts while some are just daily dying of anger-associated illnesses. Many cannot even form meaningful relationships due to the extent of the rejection and damage that their experiences have left them with, while others never have partners.

The Moabite and Ammonite curse of incest has been plaguing generation after generation. Nevertheless, we are so grateful that we do not have to remain under those curses because when Jesus came, it was to set the captives free. We who are redeemed by the blood of Jesus know that we are under no such curses for who the son sets free is free indeed .

BREAKING GENERATIONAL CURSES OF INCEST

We break generational curses of incest in our immediate families and from our bloodline in the name of Jesus. We loose those that are bound through this stronghold and we cast rejection out of their bloodline, we cast anger out of their spirits, we release their souls and we fill them with the joy of Jesus. We loose them from every curse of inferiority, of resentment, and of emptiness and we ask the Lord to take every pain and hurt from their lives.

In addition, every empty space that has been left in their spirit, soul, and body, we fill with the everlasting love of Jesus and the peace of God that passeth every human understanding. They are no more under those bondage, thank God they are free at last, in the name of Jesus.

INCEST AND RAPE IN THE FAMILY LEADING TO REJECTION

And it came to past that Absalom the son of David had a fair sister whose name was Tamar and Amnon the son of David loved her. And Amnon was so vexed that he fell sick for his sister Tamar for she was a virgin. 2 Samuel 13:1-2

And Amnon said unto Tamar, bring the meat unto the chamber that I may eat of thy hand. And Tamar took the cakes, which she had made and brought them into the chamber to Amnon her brother. And when she brought them unto him to eat, he took hold of her, and said unto her, come lie with me my sister. And she answered him, nay my brother, do not force me for no such thing ought to be done in Israel. Do not thou this folly.

And I whither shall I cause my shame to go? And as for thee thou shalt be as one of the fools in Israel. Howbeit he would not harken unto her voice, but being stronger than her, he forced her, and lay with her. 2 Samuel 13:10-14

The example in the passage above is probably the most sickening form of rape and incest. The brother desired his blood sister so much that he developed a beastly lust that culminated in her rape. The name Tamar means palm tree and we are told that she was a very beautiful lady.

One would have expected that a brother with such a beautiful sister would want to protect her from rape and would do his utmost to ensure that she is married to the most perfect of husbands. If he had really wanted her for himself, that in itself would have been a sin. However, the bible shows us that he did not really want her for himself, he just didn't want another man to have her as a virgin.

As the story progresses, we learn that having raped his sister, Amnon then cast her out into the street. She felt so hurt and rejected that she dressed herself in mourning clothes and locked herself away from everyone.

At least Lot's girls had the decency to get their father drunk so that he could not witness their incest. Amnon, in contrast, had no integrity whatsoever. There are many family members who have inherited this Amnon curse of rape and they have neither conscience nor integrity with it.

As children of God we are constantly being told to feel sorry for these individuals because it is the work of Satan in their lives. I am not saying that Satan is not at work. On the contrary, I know that he is constantly destroying the lives of God's children.

However, many of those folks were born and bred in the pew, and some have listened to biblical teachings all of their lives. However, when they should be servants and leaders in the Church of Christ, like the backslidden Israelites they are forever giving room to the enemy in their lives.

Many of our women and men who should be carrying high the banner of Jesus Christ are very wounded. They are so broken, so empty and feel so unwanted and unloved that we cannot even get them to sit in the church and to listen to the word of God. They are constantly asking the question:

 Why me? Lord, where were you when all of these were happening to me?

I need the people that have asked themselves these questions to know that God saw when those things were happening but also to realise that He warned us that the sins of our fathers and mothers will pass on to the third and fourth generations.

Unfortunately, although you do not know what your ancestors did, you have become the victim, but we thank God, that He is truly ready to release you and to set you free. He is ready to prepare you for that home where those sins will be remembered no more for He will be your protector forever.

It is really a shame to know that there are born again Christians in churches who are lusting after their family members and are committing incest and rape. Many of our children are suffering and dying in silence.

BREAKING THE CURSE OF AMNON

We break the curse of Amnon out of our bloodline in the name of Jesus.

We call our broken brothers and sisters who have been victims of incest and rape to the throne room of Christ, and we break every rejection from over their lives. We continue to set them free, free from the Moabite curse, free from the Ammon curse and free from the curse of Amnon in the name of Jesus. We also cover them in the precious blood of Jesus.

THE CURSE OF POLYGAMY

But King Solomon loved many strange women, together with the daughter of pharaoh, women of the Moabites, Ammonites, Edomites, Zidonians and Hittites.

Of nations concerning which the Lord said unto the children of Israel, ye shall not go in to them; neither shall they come in unto you. For surely they will turn away your hearts after their gods. Solomon cleaves unto these in love.

And he had seven hundred wives, and princesses and three hundred concubines. And his wives turned away his heart from God. 1 KINGS 11:1-3

In the case of King Solomon, we find that a single human being had seven hundred wives and princesses and three hundred concubines. I believe that it was only by the grace of God that he was able to see old age. It almost seems as if Solomon did not want other men to have wives.

In addition, the Lord had warned his people against the kinds of women that Solomon slept with. If we examine the backgrounds of these women, we find that some were Moabites and Ammonites who were Children of incest, and that others were Hittites, Edomites and Zidonians, who worshipped Baal and were therefore buried in idolatry.

Therefore, not only did Solomon possess an ungodly and beastly lust, but he was also disobedient. Because of his sin, nations and nations have inherited this curse and untold curses and sufferings have befallen mankind.

In addition, one can only imagine the kind of jealousy and resentment that must have existed amongst his ladies, because within that kind of polygamous household there must be a lot of competition for the most favourable position. So we find that what is generated is spirit of anger, hatred, jealously, resentment and probably a spirit of witchcraft, as the ladies desire to impress their gentleman.

I sometimes really think about the length of time that it must have taken the Great King Solomon to go around and sleep with all of his concubines, princesses, and wives, and I think that this is disgraceful.

Many times, I have heard ladies from polygamous backgrounds saying things like:

Oh, it s acceptable in my culture.
I don t mind being in a polygamous relationship.

They try to justify this argument by saying that at least they know that they are safe from venereal infections, because they know the other partners.

Ladies just you listen to me. I will never share my husband with another woman! That is a curse from the pit of hell and even if there are twenty of you in that relationship, your husband has inherited a lust curse from the lineage of the great King Solomon. Therefore, even if he had a hundred of you he would still go looking for another three hundred. Moreover, does he take each new lady to be tested for venereal infections?

This is a manifestation of a generational curse that comes through the bloodline and is only acceptable because you have allowed it and accepted it. I can just imagine that when the man cannot make the rounds then the ladies will turn to the ladies for affection and so we have lesbianism developing.

God made two perfect human beings whom He placed in the garden of Eden. He made a man called Adam and a lady called Eve. He didn t create Adam and Eve, Sarah, Mary, Joan et cetera to go with him. Therefore that is only a cover-up for infidelity. It is truly no wonder there are such diseases as AIDS.

Ladies respect yourselves and walk away from this situation if you are in it. No decent woman would want to take second place in a relationship.

No wonder our men are not in the churches, the fact is, they are too busy searching for ladies and they know that in the eyes of God that is sin. Furthermore, we have a name for it in our society; it is called bigamy and you can still go to prison for it.

POLYGAMY THROUGH THE GENERATIONS

And unto David were sons born in Hebron. And his firstborn was Ammon of Ahinoam the Jezreelite. And his second Chileab of Abigail, the wife of Nabal, the Carmelite. And the third Absolam the son of Maacah the daughter of Talmai, king of Geshur. 2 Samuel 3:1—5

This chapter has named six of David s wives. In fact there were three other wives that are not mentioned here, David had nine listed wives. In the same book, we are later informed that:

He took more concubines and wives out of Jerusalem, after he had come from Hebron. 2 Samuel 5:13

So the bible tells us that the sins of the mother and the father visit the third and fourth generations. Here we have David taking many wives and concubines, directly out of the houses of idolatry. David, however, does not compare to his son Solomon. I doubt that any other person in history has surpassed him.

As we trace the bloodline, we continue to see how these sins passed on through generation after generation. Rehoboam, Solomon s son had seventy-eight wives and concubines and his son Abijah had fourteen wives. (2 Chronicles 11: 8 and 13:21)

BREAKING THE CURSE OF POLYGAMY

We break the curse of polygamy from the bloodline and we call our men and women into relationships that are pleasing and acceptable to God. We call our men back to repentance and bring them to the throne room of God were they will receive grace and mercy. We loose our ladies out of polygamous relationships and call their minds back to the Lord, in the name of Jesus.

THE CURSE OF LESBIANISM AND HOMOSEXUALITY

And they called Lot And said unto him, where are the men that came in to thee this night bring them out to us so that we might have sex with them. Genesis 19: 5

There was a certain Levite who took to him a concubine out of the house of Bethlehem, Judah. And the concubine played the whore against him and went to his father s house . And her husband arose and went after her to

speak friendly unto her and to bring her back and when they were by Jebus the day was far spent. And the servant said unto the master come, I pray thee and let us turn in to the city of the Jebusites that we might lodge there But the man would not harken unto them so the man took his concubine and brought her forth unto them and they abused her until the morning and when the day began to spring they let her go. JUDGES 19

Here we have another dreadful story of abuse and rape. In both cases, the men wanted to sleep with men and did not ask for the ladies. Both curses stem form the generation of the people of Sodom and were known as Sodomites in Hebrew. It is from this word that we have the word Sodomy meaning homosexuality.

In the first example, the beastly depravity of these men meant that they preferred the angels than the human being. In the second, they did not ask for the lady although they had seen her. They wanted to have a homosexual affair with the man.

The man would not go out to them and instead he sent out his girl friend. A decent man would rather die than to send his lady out to those beasts. It is no wonder that the lady had to run away from such a coward.

Moreover, not only was he a coward but he was also a wicked person, for how could he do such a thing? In current times therefore we are not surprised to find that some men continue to be filled with this ungodly lust for each other.

Many say that it has to do with the genes. Even if the genes have been misinformed at some point during conception, this is because of the inherent generational curse that runs through that family s bloodline. It is a stronghold that needs to be dealt with and to be broken, otherwise, there will be no escape for that person.

For those of us with an unforgiving nature please remember that we are not God, and God is not a man that he should lie. He says that heaven and earth shall pass away but none of His words will pass.

I know that some of us will have difficulties forgiving the homosexual priests and the lesbian nuns. However, we all will need to pray for them. They will need to understand that God said that we should get married have children and replenish the earth. However, I do not know why anyone would think that there is one set of rules for them and one for all other Christians. Homosexuals and lesbians have no place in the kingdom of heaven. They need help and I pray for them right now that the Lord will begin to break those ancestral curses out of their bloodlines and set them free in the name of Jesus.

GENERATIONAL CURSE OF COVETOUSNESS AND DECEPTION

And it came to pass in an eventide that David arose from off his bed and walked upon the roof of the King s house. And from the roof he saw a woman washing herself. And the woman was very beautiful to look upon and David sent messengers and took her and she came in unto him. 2 Kings 11:2 & 4

It was out of this very relationship between David and Bathsheba that king Solomon was conceived. Bathsheba was the wife of a Hittite and David obtained her through lust, covetousness, and murder. As the story unfolds, David arranges the death of Uriah in order to get his wife. God was so angry that he brought a curse unto David s household and the child died that was conceived through that first union.

When David pleaded with the Lord for forgiveness, the Lord told him in the same chapter that he would take the curse off him and place it on his wives and his generation.

GENERATIONAL CURSE OF LIES, DECEPTION, WITCHCRAFT

The final set of curses we shall look at, are known as the Jezebel curses.

And it came to pass that when Jezebel heard that Naboth was stoned, and was dead, that Jezebel said to Ahab, arise, take possession of the vineyard of Naboth the Jezrelite, which he refused to give thee for money. For Naboth is not alive but dead. 1 Kings 21:15

Now Jezebel was the daughter of Ethbaal who was the king of the Zodians. The Zodians directly worshipped Baal and studied the Zodiacs, and had no part with God. Jezebel means fornication and unmarried. Ahab was an Israelite and Ahab married the daughter of Baal. He therefore had adopted all the lies, witchcraft and deception from Jezebel.

The bible tells us of a man called Naboth who had a vineyard. Ahab was a wealthy king who one day looked across his fence, saw the vineyard, and decided that he would have it. With the help of his wicked wife, they were able to have Naboth stoned to death and then they stole his vineyard. As such this vineyard was obtained through lies deception, murder, force and covetousness.

These are some rampant strongholds in the lives of our people that have caused so much death and wickedness in our society. And the only way that we can come into God s true purpose for our lives is by breaking those sickening generational curses out of our bloodline.

The people of Israel practised all these evils and they have been passed on through the bloodline and from generation to generation. They are generational curses, and for the current generations, many of these curses are just the norm, and it is hard for them to do any thing else. These curses have come through to us from ancient days.

As Christians, we all need to have a thorough understanding of the will of God for our lives. Only when we are aware of this, can we begin to operate in our true purpose and calling. Moreover, when we begin to do so, we will be able to do exploits for the kingdom of God and against dark forces.

These kinds of curses are blockages to our true spiritual growth. Can you imagine someone living comfortable in a polygamous household and claiming that he is the best of Christians? Or a sister or brother who sits in a congregation all puffed up and angry and filled with jealousy and resentment against the next sister or brother who might be able to buy a better suit than they could?

Imagine members of the assembly who is supposed to be happily married and yet they sit in the pew pretending to be worshipping God and to be holier than thou. At the same time they are filled with lust for brothers or sisters from the same assembly. While they are supposed to be focusing their minds on Jesus, their hands are in the air but their minds are on the church member.

It is no wonder that there are so many dry church services that are packed with so called worshippers, but the anointing is absent from the assembly. And instead of the presence of God we find curses and strongholds of lust, anger, envy, maliciousness, covetousness, resentment, polygamy, you name them. We are no better than the ancient children of Israel.

Our churches are empty of the men; most of them are too busy looking for partners. Our ladies are too shy and hurting to come into the midst of the congregation and to celebrate Jesus with us. They are victims of the Amnonic and Ammonic curses.

We are still under the Canaanite curse of murder, and jealousy, the Ammonite, and the Moabite curse of incest. The Zebusite, Perizite, and the Hittites curses of idolatry and witchcraft are influencing us. We transport through our bloodline the

Solomon curse of polygamy and the Jezebel spirit of adultery. Some have the Sodomy spirit of homosexuality and Lesbianism.

We have too many Jezebel spirits in our midst. We worship the Lord with hands that are too heavy to lift in the air to give Him the Glory. Our churches are filled with strongholds and yet we daily pray that God will bring back the Glory.

Why do we believe that the Glory of the Lord will penetrate through filth? We want to begin to clean up our lives and our churches before we can ask for the glory of the Lord to descend in our midst and in our lives.

I believe that God is about to show His Glory upon this land, as we have never seen it before. Nevertheless, He needs His people to be cleansed from the uncleanness that they have inherited. Only then will He be able to pour out His glory upon them, and man will truly see that God is still in the business of working miracles.

For too long we as the chosen people have been burdened. We have been going around with shackles on our feet, on our hands and around our necks. We are not even walking, we are crawling. However, God wants to equip us with wings so that we will no longer walk, but instead we will fly. We will mount up with wings like an eagle.

Satan knows that it is in the house of the Lord that our boys and girls become ladies and gentlemen and so he has placed so many curses and strongholds in their lives and is keeping them away.

It is in the church that our jobs are sorted out, and where our marriages, and our finances are sorted out. It is where we receive healing from illnesses, it is where the curses are being broken and where we will find the peace and contentment that we need to carry on in a world which is riddled with sin, conflict and diseases.
 The devil is trying to hide the truth from God s children. He is well aware of the joy that awaits them in the house of the Lord. Therefore, he tries to keep them out, from reaching into God s promise land and from entering a place of joy, hope and refreshment in Christ Jesus. As Satan fights on, so is our Lord finding ways of making sure that those that are bound be loosed from the shackles and shame of sin, for He came to set the captives free.

Chapter 18

Curses in the Form of a Spell

And the Lord God said unto the serpent, because thou hast done this, thou art cursd above every beast of the field: Upon thy belly thou shalt go, and dust shalt eat all the days of thy life.Genesis 3:14

MANIFESTATIONS OF CURSES

We have already looked at the story of Satan beguiling Eve, and thus allowing man to be able to discern between good and bad. God, in his anger, placed a curse upon the evil one so that he became a serpent that crawls upon its belly, and placed enmity between the serpent and women.

The devil is well aware of how to place a curse upon anyone because he was the first in the scriptures to have a curse placed upon him. Therefore, throughout history, he continues to find counterfeits for whatsoever God does. Of course, he would love to measure up to our supreme God, but as mentioned earlier, the creation cannot challenge the creator.

Thanks be to God we know that anything that is counterfeit does not last. It reveals itself after a while, corrodes, and then wears away. Anything that God does is permanent, and only He has the power to change every plan of Satan.

A witch belongs to the devil s kingdom and is someone who has been trained in the area of casting spells upon an individual. He knows how to use the spoken word to place a curse.

I remember that as a youngster growing up in Jamaica I was a hard childhood. I was the youngest in a family of twelve; I had six brothers who were fighters and I came behind a line of four tough boys who were always fighting.

I therefore learned how to fight from quite a young age and gained respect from my pairs. The elders were accustomed to rebuking children and would sometime flog those children that they deemed to be rude on the streets and would then send them home to their parents. In most cases, these children could not tell their parents that they were flogged for most often they would receive another flogging on top of that which they had previously received.

Nevertheless, those elderly folks knew that I was one child that they could not flog. After all, I did not feel that they had any authority to do so, because they were not my parents. Therefore, they kept their distance where I was concerned, and I must say that I had quite a few enemies because of that.

We were told as kids growing up who were the most feared iniquity workers in the community and our parents often warned us to keep our distance from them. I always felt that God was responsible for us and that only He had the power to hurt us so I continued with my boldness.

I remember at that time that children usually sat for the common entrance examination, and the result in our district was generally one to nil yearly. We were told that this was due to the notorious community obeah man, who was making sure that children did not pass their exams.

At about eleven years of age, I had an experience, which will forever live, in my memory. I was attending a summer school at the local Methodist church hall, and I noticed that a group of people was frequently gathered at the home of the local obeah man. We were told that he was dying and was confessing his sins and out of curiosity, I stopped by one evening to see what was happening.

I saw a very frail, small man who looked very ill and tormented. In addition, he stank of faeces. He was trying to get out of the house while folks were trying to retain him. As he pushed forward, he was asking people who they were and were telling them what evil he had done either to them or to their family members.

When he asked me who I was, he told me that all he had done to my brothers was to pass his hands through their hair and that they had no choice but to become failures. Of course, most of my elder brothers did not make much of life and two had died quite young.

There was a very huge rock at a corner of the community s centre and I heard him say that he had planted some demonic things under that rock. He said that he did this so that all the boys in the community would lean on it and that they would become worthless. Sure enough, hardly anyone who sat on that rock had made anything of him or herself. That rock still sits as ugly as ever, in its place until this day and everyone is afraid of going near it.

At one stage of his confession, I heard him asking for the opportunity to go up to the local primary school. He said that he wanted to remove the destructive things that he had buried under it. These he claimed had impeded the progress of the children at that school. Shortly after making his horrid confessions, this man died. The building was knocked down and a new one was built, and sure enough, after that children began to pass their exams.

I cannot say exactly what impact this experience had on me, but my parents removed me from that community shortly after and I continued my education in another part of the country.

When I graduated from high school, I went back home to live for a while in the same community, during which time I applied for higher studies.

One evening, as I was passing the local shop I smelled the sweet scent of cakes baking in the air, and I jokingly said to the shopkeeper:

When you are baking those beautiful cakes, you do not give your customers any of them!

I went for a walk and returned to the shop shortly after and to my surprise; there she was with this lovely delicious looking piece of cake in her hand, which she handed me.

I was very surprised and I remember telling her that I had been joking and tried to refuse the cake because my parents did not allow me to eat from people. However, she insisted that I take the cake, and she was very persuasive. After eating it I felt fine at first, but after a short while I felt like I had died a thousand deaths. I began to burp loudly as though my stomach was packed with fizz, and when I did, it stank.

I became quite sick with my stomach, but the doctor could not find out what was wrong with me and the x-rays did not show anything. At that time I was due to go into teacher s college and for days I lay in bed being unable to move. I began to loose weight and my digestive system began to deteriorate to the extent that I could not eat anything soluble.

My parents had exhausted taking me to the doctors who could not diagnose an illness. It was when I was very badly gone that I went to bed one night and had a vision of what to do and when I awoke and shared the vision with my mother she did what I was told to do, and I then began to recover. It was only through God s mercies that I was able to make it through.

On another occasion, I came home from work one evening to see a crowd of people that had congregated at the gate of the village butcher. When I asked what that meant, I was told that stones were being thrown at the house and that no one knew where they were coming from. We all found this quite weird, but very exciting. In my curiosity, I joined the crowd; I really wanted to prove for myself that stones were being thrown from nowhere.

As my friends and I stood there wondering whether we would witness this strange activity, sure enough, a stone came out of nowhere, flew past my ear and into the front window of the house.

Suddenly, my anxiety turned into fear and we all looked around apprehensively to see where the stones were coming from, but there was nothing to indicate that anyone was guilty of throwing the stones.

As time progressed, the local born again Holy Ghost Filled pastor was called. He was a mighty man of God and was more like the community doctor. If he prayed for you and you did not recover, then you could almost call in the priest. He came and was nearly knocked over with stones. He took his other ministers and left saying that this was more than he could manage.

While all of this was happening the lady of the house was cooking her food and she found that when she went to check her pot it was filled with kerosene oil. Her baby's skin began to shred from its body and all sorts of dreadful things were happening in the house. The baby was soon hospitalised and people came from far and near to see her.

In one of the rooms there was a crippled man who usually sat in a chair near to the door. One morning as my niece went to the standpipe to fetch water, she ran back home to tell us that there was a weird looking smoke coming from the house.

When we went there, it was all like something out of a horror movie. The man who was paralysed and could not speak, rose from his chair and a horrifying shout of fire came from his throat. We all stood and watched as the house burned to the ground. The walls are still standing today as witness to that dreadful demonic occurrence that took place at that house.

Shortly after this, the family left the community in disgrace. We were told that they had migrated to the USA. These people had pretended to be Christians, but were involved in heights of iniquity and God showed them a sign, which they will never forget.

We were informed that they had belonged to a high order secret cult in America and that when they could not pay their fees, a spell had been cast upon them and that principalities had been sent to take care of them.

There are many stories of such happenings in villages all around the world, but such things are rarely spoken of. People prefer to write about good things than to make mention of the works of the Kingdom of darkness.

However, it is important that you realise that these things do exist. That is why the Apostle Peter tells us that we should be vigilant and be sober for the enemy, as a roaring lion, goes about seeking those that he may devour.

These spells are always unfruitful for the person that casts them, however, as the old man who made those horrid confessions had a nasty end to his life, as did the person who gave me that piece of cake.

When these spells are cast on anyone, it is generally to ruin their lives, and only the Lord in His mercy can remove those curses from the lives of His children. I was once afraid of such evils things, but now I know that God has not given me the spirit of fear, but of power, of love and of a sound mind. When we are in Christ, we know that we are dwelling in the secret place of the most High and that we are hiding under the shadows of the wings of the Almighty.

We are aware that we are not merely visitors, but that we are dwelling in the secret place. Consequently, we are not afraid of neither curses nor spells, for our God is a consuming fire and is able to consume all the forces that might come up against us.

THE DIFFERENCE BETWEEN CURSES & DEMONIC POSSESSION

It is sometimes very difficult to differentiate between a curse and demonic possession as the latter can often come in the form of the former. For example, a person can place a curse on someone that would include that a demon takes over the life of the person. On the other hand, a curse can be passed on from generation to generation in what is termed a generational curse as discussed in the last chapter.

In cursing another person, one can place a curse that endures throughout the family line, and which passes through to the third and fourth generations, and even to successive ones. David discharged generational curses upon his enemies in many of the Psalms.

One example is Psalm 109 as where he says the following:

Let his children be fatherless and his wife a widow. Let his children be continually vagabonds and beg. Let them seek their bread also out of their desolate places.

Let the extortioner catch all that he hath and let the stranger spoil his labour. Psalms 109

Further on in the same passage he continues,

Let his posterity be cut off and in the generation following let their names be blotted out.

This is a most frightening Psalm, but it also serves to remind us that there are blessings and there are curses and that we should be very careful how we treat people in this world. As children of God we need to be aware that there are still men and women of God who will repeat this Psalm against their enemies when under oppression by them.

I would however remind those of us who are Christians that vengeance belongs to the Lord. In addition they should be reminded of the wise words of King Solomon in the book of proverbs that says:

When a man s ways please the Lord, He maketh even his enemies to be at peace with him. Proverbs 16:7

Furthermore, those who are casting curses should consider the innocent children who might have not been in this world when their parents were oppressing them. Even if they had been around, they should not be responsible for the wrongdoings of their parents. Proverb also tells us that:

Undeserved curse will not come to rest. (Pr. 26: 2).

Let us briefly look at the story of Balaam in the book of Numbers.

The bible tells that the Israelites had entered into their promise land and that they were conquering everything that lay in their path. No matter how huge and ferocious the opposing tribe was, it would be defeated.

They had pitched in the plains of the Moabites, and as such they were evidently preparing to make war with them. They had just defeated the Amorites and this was such a defeat that the Moabites became afraid of them. They realised that the Israelites had a supernatural power with them.

Balaak, who was the ruler of the Moabites, realised that physical strength alone could not overcome them. Being knowledgeable in idolatry and in the casting of spells through the placing of a curse, he asked for someone who had the power to cast a spell upon the Isrealites.

We learn that Balaam had the gift upon his lips of pronouncing both blessings and curses. He was so notorious that although he lived in a far away land, Balaak sent mules of treasures to him to entice him into coming to the land of Moab to curse the Israelites.

Balaam was a godly man and had to be given directives by God to do pronounce curses, and so in Numbers 22:8, we read that he told the King s messengers:

Lodge here this night and I will bring you word again as the Lord shall speak unto me.

Balaam consulted with the Lord who told him,

Thou shalt not go with them, thou shalt not curse the people for they are blessed.

Balaam obeyed the Lord and told the messengers that he could not curse them. In response to this, the king sent back more treasures. This time the treasures enticed Balaam and so he went back to the Lord to see if He could change His mind. He knew that what the Lord says that He will do, that He will do and, and that which He says He will not do he will not do. Nevertheless, because of greed Balaam went back to ask.

Finally, he was given leave to go. However, even though he went, he still had to prophesy blessings upon the people, because those whom the Lord has blessed no man can curse.

When the Lord blesses you, Mohammed can t curse you, Buddha can t touch you, Harry Krishna cannot come near you, for those whom the Lord blesses, no man can curse.

They can throw the greatest witches party, call up every legion in hell and cast the best spell ever imagined. As children of God we are comprehensively insured by the blood of Jesus, and we are fully loaded. Therefore, rejoice in the Lord and again I say rejoice.

I would like to pause here to say, that there are many people in this world who exist like vagabonds, and who seem to be constantly living as though under the influence of a spell and just cannot understand why.

They make no money for themselves and even when they do, they feel as if they labour in vain as they cannot account for their earnings, which always seem to melt away from them.

Some cannot hold down a job, and in some cases even though they have the best qualifications they just cannot be employed. They always appear as though they are in another world, always seem lost worried and fearful, and just cannot seem to put their lives into perspective. These folks may well be living under the influence of a generational curse. We give thanks to God, however, because we know that although we may walk through the valley of the shadow of death we will fear no evil. Because we know that:

JESUS CAME TO SET THE CAPTIVES FREE!

If you fall into this category, I want you to know that you do not have to carry those burdens anymore because the blood of Jesus was shed to redeem you from the curse of the enemy. Right now I would just like you to pause for a moment to pray this prayer.

A PRAYER FOR DELIVERANCE FROM CURSES AND BONDAGE

Father in the name of Jesus, I pray that you release me from every generational curse, from every oppression and from every force that is keeping me from realising my true potential. I plead the blood of Jesus over my life, I plead the blood of Jesus over the lives of my family members, and I loose them from every generational curse.

Everything that Satan is holding for me in the realm of darkness I take back by force right now in the name of Jesus. I take back my happiness, my wealth, my health and my prosperity. Everything that he is holding that belongs to my family members I take back by force right now in the name of Jesus.

Father I thank you for your blood that has redeemed me from bondage, from every yoke and from every plan of darkness. Father I give you thanks for a new life. I give thanks for a life, which is filled with success, with joy, with happiness, with good health and abundance, in the name of Jesus.

I now stake my claim under the shadows of the wings of the Almighty and in the secret place of the most High God. I now release all anger, hurt pain, unforgiveness, resentment and any other form of evil that has been weighing me down throughout my life.

I now take the authority and I kick the enemy out of life and I search for every open door of sin, which will allow him access to my life, and I close them in the name of Jesus.

I declare that I now belong to Jesus and that the enemy has no place in my life. I am now free, in the name of our Lord Jesus.

Amen

You should pray this prayer and lift your faith knowing that God has been waiting for you to pray this prayer for a long time. He wants you to trust in Him, to take your burdens to Calvary, and to leave them there. You have just taken those years of heavy burdens to Jesus. Please leave them at His feet and trust in Him to take them from you and to change all of that darkness into light.

THE POWER OF THE TONGUE

David was a praying man. However, he did not only pray, he also made use of the spoken word. Proverb tells us that:

Death and life are in the power of the tongue. PROVERBS 18:21

We therefore ought to be very careful of what we say because we can speak blessings or curses over the lives of individuals and over our lives. I have heard many parents telling their children that they are worthless and that they will not make anything of themselves in life. That is a curse and more often than not, those words that are spoken over the lives of children actually come to pass.
How many of us have said something very negative about someone, only to find

that exactly what we said about that individual comes to pass. We then begin to feel sorry that we had uttered such negative things about that person s life.

The spoken word is like a seed that has been planted which is often germinated by negative thoughts. We must learn to speak words of comfort, love, and peace, healing, prosperity, abundance, health and happiness over our lives and our circumstances. In so doing we are planting positive seeds, which should be nurtured, and watered with wonderful and rich thoughts.

There are so many people in this world that daily curse themselves without realising it. We continually tell ourselves what we cannot do, where we cannot go, what we cannot obtain. It is always I cannot, I cannot, I can t. We need to retrain our minds and to focus on the following:

We can do all things through Christ who strengthened us.

CHARMS AND AMULETS

He that dwelleth in the secret place of the most High shall abide under the shadows of the Almighty. PSALMS 91:1

Most of the people who came to see me when I was involved in psychic readings, came because they felt that they needed some form of protection from evil. They also wanted some type of charm to make them successful. I could have given them absolutely anything and they would have gone away feeling safe and secure. Even though I had read many books on charms and amulets there was no way that I was going to give people those things to drink or to wear on their bodies.

On most occasions I would write out a psalm on paper and place it neatly in a bag, which I would tightly seal while telling them that there was power in the bag that they were carrying. Sure enough they would feel that those pieces of paper were protecting them.

Sadly, there are thousands of people in the world who are being fooled by little pieces of papers with some weird writings on them. They are also being fooled by stones or rings, which are supposed to possess supernatural powers. If only those poor folks knew that true power lies only in the Name of Jesus, in the Blood of Jesus and in the power of the Holy Ghost.

The things that are given to those poor victims who go looking for protection can be so evil that in many cases they will enable an evil spirit to take over the body of the individual. This is something that I have come across in my Ministry.

Let us take, for example, the notorious protection ring. A protection ring is something that is generally loaded with quicksilver, which is otherwise known as mercury, or which is sometimes loaded with things from the graves of the dead. In the case of mercury, it is widely known that this is a very dangerous metal. It is so poisonous that the thermometers that are used to contain it are now being discarded. This is something that can seep through the pores into the skin and can poison the blood, thus killing the individual.

I have heard of people who have died wearing these things, and that doctors have been unable to tell the reason for their death. Occultists have also been known to give mercury to the individual to drink and in most cases they will never tell their victims what they are giving to them. This poisonous substance is said to be able to protect the individual from evil.

I would say that this is one of the most evil things in occultic practice. I have encountered many a poor soul with this liquid inside of them and most of these individuals have large bulging stomachs and suffer great pain.

They also suffer from indigestion and what the doctor would classify as irritable bowel syndrome. I suspect that this very harmful substance would stay inside the individual and gradually seep into the blood stream, eating away at the internal organs until it eventually kills the person.

If a person is wearing something that is taken from a grave, then most obviously, they are inviting demons around them. In addition, these individuals are generally amongst those that are possessed by evil spirits.

In making talismans and amulets, witches generally do all sorts of demonic incantations to charge these things with the presence of evil. Therefore the only protection that the person/s wearing these can get are from the kingdom of darkness and these forces are just not capable of protecting anyone. Their job is to create destruction and complete havoc in the lives of people. It is very sad to know the depths of sin and filthiness that some will sink to in the quest for power and protection.

We often look at the ordinary man or woman who is struggling in this life and we want to believe that they are the ones who would go looking for protection and power. However my experience with the media has shown me that some of the most disturbed people and those seeking protection and power are those that are in public life.

If only these people could truly understand that these things that they are doing are not without implications. Although at the outset it would appear that they are prospering and that they are doing well, it would do well for them to know that Satan s work will never be permanent. His works are counterfeit and therefore they will not last. Furthermore, all charms and talismans have things engraved on them which are very evil and which attract the presence of evil forces to the wearers or wherever they are placed.

I fail to understand why any born again child of God should feel that there are other means by which s/he could receive deliverance and protection expect through the blood of Jesus. Nonetheless, I have been in the presence of many so-called Christians who are charged from the crown of their heads to the soles of their feet with evils that are associated with talisman and charms.

As soon as I am in the presence of people who are wearing these things, I begin to feel a heavy oppression forming around me. I am often usually able to identify these objects, warn the wearer about the dangers of wearing them and have them removed.

Once a person begins to dabble with witchcraft and occultism, they will become hooked on it. The fact is, all mediums work with unclean spirits, and as soon as you have consulted these people, you will leave and these things will leave with you.

How many people have been to see a clairvoyant or have consulted a tarot reader or medium through the telephone, only to find that as soon as they have finished with that consultation then they begin to have a desire for another one?

These people will have such an inclination to have another visit that they will begin to pay large sums of money to do so.

The enemy comes not, but for to steal, and to kill and to destroy.
St John. 10:10

The medium is inspired by Satan to charge you a large sum of money. Therefore, as your visits increase, so do your savings decrease as you continue to sow your financial seed into the kingdom of darkness.

As you seek for answers to your problems, for gain and for power through these forces, you are setting yourself up for a fall. Soon you will find that you will have to take out a bank loan or borrow money to pay for the evil works of darkness. Moreover, by the time it becomes apparent to you that you have been set up for a fall, then it would be too late. Most people only realise that they ve been conned after they become bankrupt.

Having found this out, many people often feel too humiliated to speak to anyone about it. Some of these are people who would have appeared to have their lives all mapped out. Moreover, for some of them to learn that they have been conned by someone who they did not believe to be their equal in stature nor intelligence, is often too much for them to bear. The sheer shame of this has caused many to kill themselves or to have a nervous breakdown.

The Bible cannot be wrong and this is clearly the ultimate work of the enemy, and who is to know him better than the Lord Jesus. His job is to con you, rob you, and then to take your life away from you. He has no pity for anyone. He only desires to jeer and mock you when he has finished destroying you.

Satan is still trying to prove a point to mankind and to God. He desires to prove that he has some powers, however, behind that, he lacks all authority. We thank the Lord that we know that we have mighty weapons to use against him, and not only that, we also have the authority to use those weapons.

God has taught us how to identify the counterfeit. Because we know that when we are out in the world, then we are surely exposed to the con man. Nevertheless, when we are under the umbrella of Jesus Christ, then we are taught how to test the spirit. We use the weapons of our warfare and we demolish the plans of the kingdom of darkness.

For He that is in us is greater than he that is in the world.

When we identify a spirit, which is not of God, then we should take authority over it. Moreover as children of God, we have no part with the unfruitful works of darkness.

I have met so many poor souls who have been so abused by these evil workers that it is only God s grace and mercy that has kept them. I am reminded of a young couple who were planning to open a business. They had saved very hard for this venture, and having accumulated between twenty and thirty thousand pounds they decided to seek some guidance from a clairvoyant.

I do not know if they told this evil woman what they were planning to do, but by some means or other the woman found out about this money and their plans. She told them that if they took the money to her, she would be able to do some sort of work on it so that the business would be a success.

In their ignorance, they took all of their money to this witch. When they went back to see her, she had moved from her address. The last time that I saw them, they told me that the lady was traced to an address in Canada, and that the police was dealing with the case.

This trickery is nothing more than the unfruitful works of darkness and only God can help someone who is not wealthy to come to terms with losing so much money all at once.

As we make our way through this life we must quickly come to realise that in the spirit world, the basic principles are very simple. In any spiritual dealing, we are either dealing with God or the devil. If you have not sought your help from God, and are not using scriptural practices as you seek His guidance, you will be exposing yourself to trickery from the enemy. No amount of candle burning will help you, and no trinket or amulet can deliver you from whatever you are going through. Furthermore, by seeking guidance from clairvoyants and readers you are actually inviting satan and his demons to enter your life.

We have exposed in this chapter how spells and curses are used to bring about destruction as the devil uses our desires for greed, lust or revenge to draw both ourselves and those whom we wish to hurt, deeper into the kingdom of darkness.

We should be careful that the only spirit that we seek is God s Holy Spirit, who will come into our lives when we submit our will to Him.

CONCLUSION

Let us hear the conclusion of the whole matter. 'Fear God and keep his commandments, for this the whole duty of man. ECCLESIATES 12:13

HE HAS COME TO GIVE US A NEW LIFE

As children of God, we give thanks that He gives freely to us, that we do not have to be conned into salvation, nor do we need to con anyone into receiving the Lord in his heart. We give thanks that God is here at all times to pick up those broken pieces of our lives and mend them in a way that only He can. He looks at our broken pieces of pain, hurt, sorrow, humiliation, rejection and poverty, and He just picks up all of those broken pieces and puts them back together again.

You see, God is our potter and we are the clay. We are merely vessels of clay that are handled daily by many hands. As we journey through life, these hands will inevitably leave marks and scars all over us. Because clay is a soft material, we are soft and pliable, and easily scarred and bruised. As such, the coarser the hands are that handle us, the more we as delicate beings are pushed out of shape.

The problems that we are faced with daily, the cares of life, the pain, fears, turmoil and heartaches that we go through are symbolic of the hands that handle us. Sometimes these situations will be constantly eating into our beings and wearing us down. For every trial that we go through, we are left with marks, and after having several marks on our bodies we will begin to feel very battered and bruised.

Sometimes the things that we go through in life will beat at us so badly that we become so broken and appear to be irreparable. When our heavenly father looks down upon us and sees the beautiful clay vessels that He had created, He realises that He would have to re- mould and refashion us in order for Him to be glorified through us,

Thankfully some of us can be remoulded and re-shaped, and God will take the broken pieces of our lives and put them back together again. However, when God sees some of us we look so bad that we become unrecognisable to our potter. There are so many scars, holes, swellings and bruises that are left on us as a result of the way in which life has handled us. And in order for Him to be glorified through us He has to drop us very hard, break us up into unrecognisable pieces and re-make us from nothing.

When the Lord is making us over, He will ensure that He fits us up with some new parts. So He takes the heart of stone and gives us a soft one. He takes out bad lungs and bad kidneys, bad livers and hurting stomachs and he drains our blood stream and gives us a blood transfusion. Then He places His Holy Spirit within us.

When our mastermind is finished with us we become brand new in Christ Jesus, and the new organs that He gives to us help us to forget the pains of yesterday. The new spirit that He gives us allows us to fight against all other spirits and the new blood protects and seals us until the day of Jesus Christ.

When folks who knew us before try to remind us of our past, we can feel nothing for them but sympathy, for we know that only the devil reminds a person of his/her past, because he knows that he has no future. We pray for those folks that God will rid them of the characteristics of Satan.

By the grace of God we know that our past experiences are behind us and that God has turned them around for the good so that each bad experience has now prepared us for the future. Moreover, being aware of what our pass did to us and being reminded of how tattered, bruised and unrecognisable it had left us, we begin to press. We leave the things that are behind us and we press forward. For we are happy with our new looks and as we do not want to look as ugly as we were, we hold on tightly to our Father in heaven.

We know that there is nothing that is quite as ugly as sin and the father of it. Moreover we know that his desire is to make you look like him and when he is finished with you he will destroy you. But God is not like that:

For He has come that we might have life and that we might have it more abundantly.

God is not a con artist. He is the good Shepherd and the good shepherd giveth His life for His sheep. That is why the Lord gave His life for us.

So that through death, He has destroyed him who had the power over death, that is the devil. He hath delivered those who through fear of death were all their lifetime subject to bondage. Hebrews 2:14—15

Do you think that the devil would have given his life for you? And yet we have a great High Priest who has shed His blood for us, and that blood has cancelled out the need for talismans, charms, and for contact with familiar spirits. There is power in that blood to conquer all the plans of Satan over our lives, to destroy the work of iniquity, to bless our finances, to give us jobs and to protect us. Oh the unlimited power of this wonderful blood!

If you are guilty of consulting mediums and clairvoyants, tarot readers, card readers, horoscopes, stargazers, chanellers, crystal ball readers, tea leaf readers, pendulum swingers and all the other workers of iniquity, stop and think about what you are doing. You are only drawing down destruction upon yourself and not only unto yourself, but you are also passing a curse into your family line.

We give thanks that right where you are, God is waiting at your side to forgive you of all those sins. His tender arms are stretched out to you right now. He knows why you have been to those places but He is giving you the assurance that burdens are heaped at Calvary, if you will just empty your burdens at the feet of Jesus right now. I was like you, but all that those evil things gave me was a life of destruction.

Thanks be to God, Jesus saved me from that life. He took my sins away, and not only that, He gave me something that the workers of darkness do not have, that Satan cannot get, and that money cannot buy.

He gave me His love. He gave me His peace, He has filled my life with His glory and He has beautified my presence with His Grace. Now I have joy bubbling over. God can do the same thing for you today.

HE CAN MAKE YOU WHAT HE INTENDED YOU TO BE

I write this book mainly for you because I know the pain that you are feeling. I know how battered and bruised you are. I know how much the devil has lied to you. I know that you are seeking for peace and contentment. I just want you to know that you will never find it in this world without Jesus. This world is now coming to an end and all that it has to offer is hell, death and destruction.

I write unto you with tears in my eyes as I see that hell has opened its mouth getting ready to swallow you up and only Jesus can help you. You see, at one time I had all that I felt that life could offer me, but when Satan came upon me with his hosts of hell to kill me that was when I realised that I really had nothing.

I searched for many years for what I have now. I looked to the obeah man, I looked to money, I looked to fame and to fortune and I now have just one regret and that is only that it took me so long to look to Jesus.

Each time that I approach the throne room of God I pray for you. I know that you are not responsible for the state that your life is in. I know that Satan has placed a mirage in front of your eyes. I see you on the streets selling drugs. I see you lady at the corner of some street selling your body. Young man, I see you selling your body for something that will not last, and exchanging your life for death.

I see you who are hooked on drugs, I see you working witchcraft, partaking of the unfruitful works of darkness. I see you in that relationship which is not working out, in that life of faithful concubinage and I see your tears and I hear your cry. If only the Lord could take me out of this situation! If only He would make a way for me!
I see the love that you have for Jesus; I know that you love Him. That is why you are reading this book today. I see your search for Him. I know you might think that you are too far-gone or that He does not love you, or maybe you are searching for the Lord and can t seem to find Him. I see all these things.

However, I see something else which is more vivid than everything that I have seen so far. I see the Lord, high and lifted up, and I see His glory reaching out to you. I see His hands outstretched for you. I see the soft tears falling from His eyes as He gently calls you. I see the compassion in His eyes. I know the pains that He is feeling for you, that of a loving father who cries for his only child who has gone astray.

I hear Him knocking at your heart s door and asking you in a loving and gentle voice, Will you let me in?
You are special to God; so special in fact, that He sees you as a parent sees an only child that has gone away from him. He wants to rid you of every past pain, past memory, and hope that did not materialise, scars that are deep and burning, eating at your human being, deep seated in the core of your very soul, destroying your spirit. Making you far less than God had intended you to be.

He wants to give you a new life. He wants to take you to a spiritual well of clean pure water, which is everlasting and overflowing. It is clear as crystal and filled with the healing virtues of Christ Jesus. It is there to cleanse you of all of the dirt that you have been carrying throughout your life, and to heal you of all the pains that you have been through. It is there to give you a new lease of life, which is forever filled, with the Glory of God.

He wants to take you away from the environment that you are in. He wants to take those shackles from off your feet, to lift them up from where they seem stuck in that pool of mud, to move you from that spot from which you have been unable to move and which had seemed so permanent. He wants to take you from that place of doom, of utter darkness and desolation, of torment, unfruitfulness and tears and to take you to a place of complete peace and refreshment in Him.

He wants to lead you through green pastures, where He will restore your soul. God holds the world in His hands and you are a part of this world. He has control of your future, He has your destiny mapped out in front of Him and I can picture the words written in bold over your name:

CHOSEN FOR THE PROMISE LAND.

God knew you from before you were born, when you were nothing but sperm, fighting amongst billions for survival. He separated you from the rest, killed the others and chose you so that you might come into His inheritance. It is not by chance that you are here, neither were you created to live under the control of the enemy.

It doesn t matter what evil spirit might be molesting you or have lived within you. It doesn t matter what strongholds you have had to struggle with. It doesn t matter what darkness is in front of you, what past bitter memories you are living with, or what state of mind the enemy has left you in. It doesn t matter what curse has been placed upon your life or what came through to you by your bloodline.

I am here to tell you that Jesus can fix it for you. Right now He is standing next you, just waiting to wave His arms of forgiveness over your past and to erase them from His memory. He wants to heal you right where you are but you will have to make the decision that you really want Him in your life. You have been on a dance floor for all your life, dancing slowly with the devil.

That is why you are so tired because during those years he has been draining your life away. But Jesus is waiting to restore to you all that the cankerworm has eaten and all that the palmerworm has destroyed. He is here to give you real life and life in abundance. Will you give the Lord that once in a lifetime opportunity? Will you open your heart to Him?

He is the potter and you are the clay. Like myself I know that you have been so beaten up by the waves of life that you might feel irreparable. However, just as the Lord broke me into unrecognisable pieces, rebuilt my life and gave me a wonderful new start, so, if you will allow Him to, He will do the same for you. Will you surrender to His will? If the answer is yes, please say this prayer right where you are.

A PRAYER FOR SALVATION

Father I thank you for opening my eyes to see the abundance of joy that you have waiting to give me. I thank you for opening my mind to the understanding that is in you. I thank you that all is in you I am complete. Father, I hear you knocking on my heart s door and Lord I now open it to let you in. Come into my life Lord Jesus, and be the Lord of my life.

Lord, every covenant that I have made with the devil, known and unknown, I now cancel them out with your blood.

With your blood I now cancel every ungodly tie in the spirit realm. I cancel every ungodly tie of sexual relationships, every tie of abortion, of addiction, of fraud, of lies, occultism, generational curses, false beliefs and theft. I denounce them out of my life and I invite you to come in Lord and take up your residence.
Thank you Lord for washing my sins away. Thank you for a new lease of life, in Jesus name.

Amen

In saying and believing these words, God has now given you a new life and you will no longer walk, but you will fly. You now have supernatural wings and you will mount up against the enemy with wings like an eagle, soaring high above principalities, powers, spiritual wickedness in high places and above the rulers of the darkness of this world.

By the grace of God, you are now seated in heavenly places with Jesus Christ the Lord.

END TIME TESTIMONIES

These testimonies have been graciously provided to for this book by individuals who have personally experienced God's wonderful healing and deliverance power as He so awesomely manifests himself at End Time healing and deliverance Ministry. To include all the testimonies, this volume would not be able to contain them. I have therefore selected a few to give the reader a basic feel of the healing and deliverance powers of our Lord Jesus Christ as being manifested in this ministry.

Unless otherwise stated, all names have been changed to retain confidentiality.

JANE

My name is Jane and I was born in Trinidad. At around the age of twenty, I was introduced to a church called the Spiritual Baptist Church. I was led through various rituals, one, of which, is called mourning. While I was in the ritual of mourning, a spirit man came to me and told me that I was his husband.

After I left that cult, I found it impossible to form any meaningful relationships with members of the opposite sex. My relationships would only last for about three months and during that time they would be quite stormy.

I migrated to London where I married my husband. However, after three months our relationship became very stormy, and we were constantly engaged in vicious battles.

Things became so bad that I began to look for help. I knew that I had the spirit of a cobra within me because in that church I had been initiated as a high priestess and this was a very high rank. It also meant that I had to have a high-ranking partner in the spirit world. I realised that this man spirit that had appeared to me as my husband was a cobra and also that he was very jealous of any other partners that I had. He told me that I could have no other partner but him.

I really wanted my marriage to work and I had longed to be myself again. However, this vicious demon spirit made sure that I was always angry and very miserable.

I will be forever grateful for the day that a friend introduced me to Pastor Copeland-Blake. As soon as the Cobra saw her it became very angry. Pastor Copeland offered me counselling and then deliverance. When the deliverance began, the Cobra began to manifest itself and I was released.

I really thank the Lord for my deliverance because since then I have accepted the Lord Jesus as my personal saviour. I have been baptised and filled with the Holy Spirit.

I thank God for a new life in Him.

Jane

ANN

My name is Ann and I am eleven years old. I was born deaf and as such I have always had problems with my speech.

One night my mother took me to Pastor Lona for deliverance. She prayed for me, and as she came over me and touched my ears, I felt like a bubble burst in them and slowly I began to hear.

At first everything sounded fuzzy and when she told me to say the first word, I must have said something else. But then she said Jesus and I said Jesus. Then she shouted Jesus! and I shouted also Jesus!

When I went back to school, the teachers did all they could to get me to continue to wear the hearing aids, but I refused to. Because I knew I was healed. One day they stood behind me and clapped their hands to see what I would really do. I turned around, looked at them and smiled. They were very surprised.

I thank the Lord for my healing. I am eleven years old and I am here to tell the world that Jesus is real because I have found Him for myself.

Ann

MARION

I am Marion, and I was very ill when I came to Pastor Copeland for healing. I was suffering from thrombosis and I also had other complications. I was taking ten tablets a day.

I remember sitting in the church when she walked up to me, called me from my seat, and told me of the sicknesses that I had and of my swollen legs.

At that time my legs were very swollen and I could hardly walk, and as she touched me I fell under the anointing.

I also used to feel very dizzy and had suffered from severe headaches. I had also suffered from depression and had refused to leave my house. Since I fell under the anointing, I got back up to find that all of my sicknesses were gone. God did a spiritual operation on me while I was lying there under His anointing.

I am healed, I am happy, I have the Lord. I am saved, filled with The Holy Spirit and have been baptised since.

I Thank God for victory.

Marion

GILBERT

My name is Gilbert and I was very ill when I met Pastor Copeland. I had no idea that I would need to have an operation but she was able to tell me that I would be hospitalised and also that I would be operated on.

Shortly after this I was diagnosed with cancer and was admitted to the Lewisham Hospital. I was operated on and became very sick after this operation. I began to feel both mentally and physically ill.

One morning after having a very terrible night, I was lying in the hospital bed feeling very ill when Pastor walked in along with another member of the church. She lay her hands on me and prayed for me. She commanded the sickness to leave my body and it did.

By that time, all of my hair had fallen off my head and it has now grown back. I have regained all the weight that I had lost and not only that but where I once found that I had many spiritual battles with unclean spirits, now I am able to thank God not only for my physical healing but more so for a spiritual healing.

I realise that my healing came as a complete package. Pastor Copeland introduced me to the Lord Jesus Christ and I have accepted Him as my only Saviour and since then I have been enjoying the best years of life. I am so happy with the Lord totally in charge of my life. I am now equipped with the power of the Holy Spirit and now I am able to fight my battles for I am not alone.

I have nothing to give the Lord except the highest praises.

Gilbert (Own name)

JENNIFER

It was Monday morning, 6am, when a terrible headache woke me out of my sleep. I took two painkillers and prepared for work. By the middle of the morning, I realise that the headache is still there and in fact, it has been there all morning.

Tuesday, Wednesday, and Thursday came and the headache grew worse. No amount of painkillers would shift the pain.

At Bible study and after breaking of the fast on Wednesday, Pastor Copeland and the saints of the church prayed for me.

However, on Thursday morning, the headache was still there, and by now my neck was stiff and I could just about walk. I decided to go to my GP. My GP said I was fine, nothing to worry about, but I should go to the hospital, just in case.

I spent nine hours in total in the hospital where they performed numerous blood tests, brain & body scans and injected dye into my brain. However, they could not find out why I had a headache and could not move my neck. After the ninth hour, the doctor decided to carry out a lumbar puncture to pull fluid out of my spine.

One hour after, she was back. She sat down and explained that I had meningitis and that I needed to be admitted and put into quarantine with no human contact, unless they wore protective clothing. So many thoughts were going through my mind, like Am I going to die? Will I see my home again? What about my children?

I rang my family and I rang Pastor Lona Copeland-Blake. She prayed with me on the phone, counselled me on faith, hope and believing in the Lord Jesus. She encouraged me to pray, bless, praise, thank and lift up the Lord through this terrifying experience.

The next day, Brother Arthur, Sister. Barbara, Sister Princess, Sister Pauline and Brother. Kevin were by my bedside singing, praying and praising God.

The next morning, the consultant came round and examined me. He tested my mental state, my hearing and vision. He tested the strength in my limbs. His exact words were:

"I can t understand. You are showing no signs that you have meningitis ".

He ordered that intravenous drip which contained my medication be stopped. He explained that he was sending the specimen of my spinal fluid away to be tested before he continued treating me. As far as he was concerned, I should have been confused, my vision should have been impaired and there should have been some interference with my hearing and weakness of my limbs. But I showed none of these symptoms. Not one!

The meningitis had covered my spine and brain, but I was suffering none of the expected symptoms.

Meanwhile, I was being visited and prayed for everyday by one or more of the saints from the church.

Our Almighty Father had already intervened and started the healing process. He was also showing me His mercy and greatness because He had made me well without the use of medication, but through the use of faith, prayer, praise and acknowledgement of our Father s greatness.

He had walked with me through the valley of death, sent his faith, love and hope through Pastor Copeland and the saints of End Time Healing Ministry and saved me.

Jennifer (Own name)